1945

1945

A WORLD AT THE END OF WAR

MAX LIKIN

The
History
Press

To Nancy, Adele, and Leah

Cover image: 1945 VE Day revellers in Fleet Street, London. (Chronicle / Alamy Stock Photo)

First published 2025

The History Press
97 St George's Place, Cheltenham,
Gloucestershire, GL50 3QB
www.thehistorypress.co.uk

British Library Cataloguing in Publication Data.
A catalogue record for this book is available from the British Library.

ISBN 978 1 80399 915 9

Typesetting and origination by The History Press
Printed and bound in Great Britain by TJ Books Limited, Padstow, Cornwall

MIX
Paper | Supporting
responsible forestry
FSC
www.fsc.org   FSC® C013056

Trees for Lᵞfe

Contents

Introduction

The year 1945 marked the end of the Second World War. This cataclysmic event had no equivalent in human history. It spanned three continents, saw more men and women under arms, and caused more death and destruction than any other war. The unconditional surrender of Germany and Japan allowed no ambiguity. All vanquished nations had their homelands ravaged and political systems destroyed. Obliteration, not just capitulation, was the fate of Axis powers.

As much as we think of 1945 as the end, it was also a year of significant beginnings. In retrospect, 1945 announced important progress in nuclear medical science. It created international institutions to manage peace and stop wars of aggression, such as the United Nations and the Nuremberg Principles, to punish crimes against humanity. That same year quickened decolonization in Asia and Africa and it sparked important cultural shifts for women across many parts of the globe.

Conveying the conduct and experience of this pivotal year in a compact book is a challenge. Overarching themes and broad topics compete with minor facts for posthumous attention. Because wars are won on the battlefield, it is only natural that military campaigns and battles receive extensive notice, paying rightful tribute to human courage and sacrifice. Yet it is also sometimes useful to bring into focus far-flung elements and incongruous incidents that reflect the daily experiences of less-visible supporting characters.

I was walking through rows of stacks in a research library when my curiosity prompted me to pick up a war memoir from an American soldier by the name of J. Ted Hartman. Leafing through the book, it was hard to stop reading. Here was a young tank driver caught in the Battle of the Bulge on his first day of combat. Obeying strict orders, he was trying to do his best and live another day. This type of 'in the moment' history led me to other memoirs and biographies. They gave me the desire to retrace 'lived experience', not merely rational thoughts, but also primary emotions, widely shared innate feelings (joy, fear, sadness, anger, surprise, disgust). Rather than focus strictly on men and military doings, ideas on art, gender, and culture ought to be included. This is how larger-than-life personalities, such as Eleanor Roosevelt in the United States, Frida Kahlo in Mexico, and Svetlana Alliluyeva (Stalin's daughter) in the USSR, came to gain prominence in this narrative.

Sketching idiosyncratic moments up to Victory in Europe Day on 8 May, in Russia on 9 May, and in Asia on 15 August, we can see that the conflict did not end on those momentous dates. The Allies still had to find a way to punish the perpetrators and their accomplices. As wartime propaganda offices were closed in September 1945, inchoate feelings of trauma and collapse surfaced simultaneously in triumphant and defeated nations.

The nineteenth-century Russian writer Leo Tolstoy in *War and Peace* famously asserted that victories owed much to lowly, invisible characters (such as *muzhiks* or peasants) doing the right thing at the right moment. By contrast, Scottish philosopher and historian Thomas Carlyle, true to his 'Great Man' theory of history, proposed that exceptional leaders, heroes, and geniuses drove historical change. The truth is more muddled. Ordinary individuals do heroic things and, conversely, mythical figureheads behave in ordinary ways. History is always open-ended.

The year 1945 came during a period when many of the great innovations in the industrial era came into widespread prominence: the telephone, railways, nuclear science, the combustion engine, chemical engineering, aircraft production, sea power, advertising campaigns, and moving images. Yet these technologies were deployed not only to secure victory but also to dehumanize, indoctrinate, and annihilate on an unprecedented scale. In essence, total war makes industrial killing possible. The most terrifying and haunting instance of industrial killing in this century remains the Nazis' attempted genocide of the Jews. The Holocaust is not merely a past event but a historical burden; one that continually deepens the shadows of human progress.

More than that, the war gave rise to new means of pursuing domination, from computer-driven signals intelligence and multifaceted covert operations to the nuclear arms race, which ushered in a much more complex and intricate era of global history. From 1945 on, a proper, considered and shared moral appraisal of our universal ties would be the key to respecting human dignity and preserving the peace everywhere.

January

On New Year's Day, the ice groans and shrieks under the tracks of J. Ted Hartman's tank in the Battle of the Ardennes. That same day, Adolf Hitler bestows the highest military medal to the most fanatical Stuka bomber pilot the world has ever seen. As they shake hands, the ace pilot starts to protest.

In what remains of Budapest, diplomat Raul Wallenberg slips on the ice in front of the Swedish hospital. Not far from the Alsatian border, a combat surgeon questions the value and veracity of anatomy drawings. In Buchenwald, a blind French Resistance fighter is locked up with 'the crazies', crawling like worms across the concrete floor.

Accompanied by his daughter, Sarah, Winston Churchill lands in Malta trying to catch his breath before the 'Big Three' Yalta Conference.

Red Army signals operators have no words to describe liberated Auschwitz.

In Mexico City, the weather is delightful. Frida Kahlo sits at her easel painting a bouquet of creamy magnolias. Light-hearted swing jazz music fills the courtyard. Svetlana Alliluyeva, Stalin's daughter, is three months pregnant and she has just moved into the lavish House on the Embankment.

In Kunming, underground Viet Minh soldiers sitting at the Café Indochine are waiting for OSS operatives to show up.

Big guns boom in the bitterly cold Battle of the Ardennes. On New Year's Day, US tank driver J. Ted Hartman is ordered to attack the village of Chenogne, located south of Bastogne. Trees are blanketed in thick snow and houses are pockmarked with craters, leaving a clearing for German *Panzerfaust* bazookas. The ice-coated roads moan under the tracks.

A fortnight earlier, in the predawn darkness and fog of 16 December 1944, the Germans caught the Allies by surprise. They had secretly marshaled 410,000 men and kept radio silence, thereby eluding the vigilance of the Ultra codebreakers. Hitler's personal gamble is to cut the Allies' logistical lines of communication by taking the

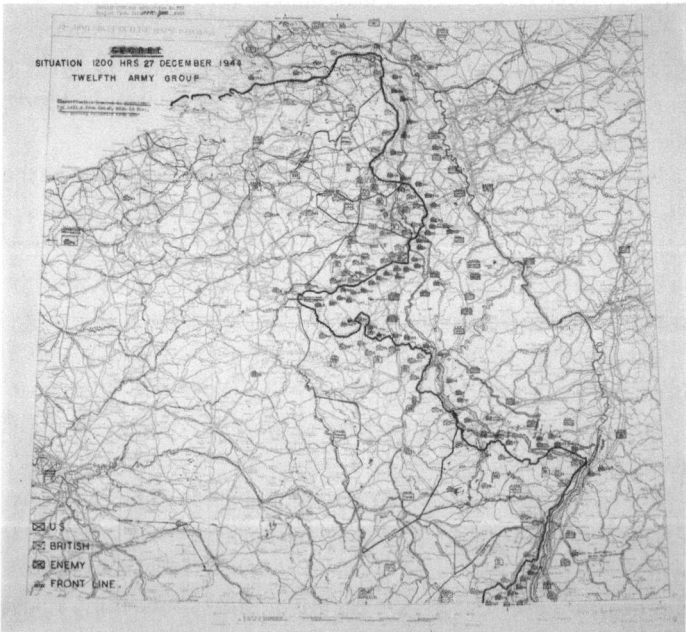

Situation 12 hours, 27 December 1944, Battle of the Bulge. (NARA NAID: 16681813 Maps and Charts)

transportation centers of Liège and Antwerp, to bring the Western leaders to the bargaining table. The attacking German force of twenty-four divisions extends some 50 miles deep and 70 miles wide.

As a simple conscript, J. Ted Hartman wants to be a good soldier. He enlisted in the Army Reserves at a recruiting station in Des Moines, Iowa, in May 1943, right out of high school. After six months of training, he was declared fit for service overseas in Europe. His point of embarkation on the East Coast was Camp Kilmer, New Jersey. At the pier, Red Cross girls gave donuts and coffee, and an army band played popular tunes.

On the night of 19 December, Hartman sailed from England to Cherbourg Harbor. At Soissons, he learned that his unit had become part of the US Third Army, under the command of General George S. Patton – wear a tie at all times and a helmet outside the tank.

At around eight o'clock on Christmas night, Hartman's tank left Soissons on a 90-mile blackout march. A French woman invited the Americans in for some hot chocolate. She refused payment but said, '*Merci*', when offered cigarettes.

Frost has formed over the interior of the thick steel walls and Hartman tries to keep his feet dry to avoid frostbite. He has cut a wool army blanket into strips 3in wide, and he changes the wrappings every few hours. On this day, his second day of action, he sees his first dead American soldier lying near his tank and wonders how humans can stand the sight.

By the end of New Year's Day 1945, the Americans are able to hold on to the village of Chenogne, which by now has lost twenty-nine of its thirty-one homes and the church. Late the next day, unexpected mortar fire explodes and Hartman sees one of his friends lifted off the ground in a standing position and fall dead on his back.

US infantrymen move along a road through Beffe, Belgium. (NARA NAID: 12010150 RG 111)

M-4 Sherman tanks lined up in a snow-covered field near St Vith, Belgium. (NARA NAID: 16730735 RG 111)

American soldiers of the 289th Infantry on their way to cut off the St Vith–Houffalize road in Belgium. (NARA NAID: 531244 RG 111)

— ◆ —

It's a fairly long drive through dark patches of pine woods. Stuka pilot Hans-Ulrich Rudel is driven past several guard posts. With close to 2,000 successful missions, Rudel is by far the best Luftwaffe pilot of all time. Wing Commander von Bülow welcomes him at the Führer's Western HQ and offers him a cup of coffee, during which the two discuss the Eastern Front.

To be on the ground is a complete waste of time, in Rudel's opinion. When landing his Stuka airplane at an airfield, his only wish is to discuss the next target for the day with other pilots and listen to a flight sergeant reporting that the airplane is refueled, repaired, and ready to go. After some desultory small talk about the situation in Hungary, Rudel follows von Bülow through several rooms and suddenly is face to face with the commanders. His mind draws a blank when he sees Hitler, except for the thought that he should have changed his shirt.

The top brass is grouped around a long table studying an oversized map. Reichsmarschall Göring is beaming. Admiral Dönitz, Field Marshal Keitel, and Colonel General Jodl scrutinize Rudel with intense curiosity. The Luftwaffe pilot should long ago have fallen from the sky, disappearing somewhere over the Eastern Front.

A corpulent Göring wedges himself forward in line with his rank of Reichsmarschall. He has a bloodthirsty grin on his face. He is a former ace fighter pilot, the recipient of the coveted *Pour le Mérite*, known as the 'Blue Max'. Right after Dunkerque, he promised Hitler that the Luftwaffe would win the war from the air and rain down fire on Britain. However, his lifelong opium addiction got much worse, and he now often dresses up in a Roman toga at his country residence at Karinhall. Built in the manner of a hunting lodge, his retreat is filled with priceless, plundered art from national museums in occupied Europe. *Der Eisener Sammler* has a weakness for masterworks depicting female nudes in mythical settings. He possesses one of the two largest art collections in the Third Reich.

The Führer offers his hand to Rudel. In recognition of his last operation, he is awarding him the very highest decoration for bravery: the Gold Oak Leaves with Swords and Diamonds. Ace flyer Rudel is promoted to the rank of group captain. In his left hand Hitler holds a black velvet-lined case. The lights in the room make the diamonds sparkle in a blaze of prismatic colors. 'Now, you have done enough flying. Your life must be preserved for the sake of our German youth and your experience.'

Rudel loudly clicks his heels, 'My Führer, I cannot accept the decoration and promotion if I am not allowed to go on flying with my wings.'

No one ever contradicts Adolf Hitler. The smile vanishes from Göring's face. The generals freeze, wondering what will happen next. The Führer looks at the ace flyer gravely, then his expression changes, 'All right, you may go on flying.' Everyone offers congratulations. We need more soldiers like him.

— ✦ —

On 13 January, Russian boots kick open the trap door in the Benczúr Street cellar. Raul Wallenberg shows his Swedish diplomatic papers, saying he must reach the highest Soviet authorities. There is now a glimmer of hope that Jewish families will no longer be rounded up. The Russians want to know why he is still in rubble-filled Pest when all the diplomats stayed in Buda. This goes on for an hour. In deserted apartments nearby, axes are hacking open parquet floors and smashing up antique furniture to collect firewood and live another day.

The Swedish diplomat's Russian is actually rather good. Belonging to a distinguished Swedish family of bankers and industrialists, Wallenberg studied Russian in high school and then architecture at the University of Michigan in Ann Arbor. As First Secretary of the Swedish

Raoul Wallenberg. (Pressenbild, Wikimedia Commons)

Embassy in Budapest, he lost no time in designing a Swedish 'protective passport'. Printed in blue and yellow and bearing the Three Crowns heraldry in the center, these official-looking documents spark tears of gratitude when they change hands. With the help of hundreds of volunteers, the Legation saved between 30,000 and 100,000 people from certain death. Some 700 Jews are now squatting on the premises of the Legation.

One day, Wallenberg will appear on commemorative stamps and street names, on scholarships, on study halls and in ritual academic debates. To be sure, war is the defeat of diplomacy. There is no room here to analyze the International Committee of the Red Cross (ICRC), whose leaders for a long time thought the Third Reich had won the war. Thus, they did not protest when trains packed with mothers and children were headed east to some unknown destination. Red Cross women in various capitals sent alarmist telegrams to the ICRC, demanding to know the cattle cars' final destinations. At one moment or another, Wallenberg was creating such a stir that the ICRC felt compelled to act. By that time, however, 1 million children had been murdered.

Wallenberg is driven in his blue Studebaker to the Russian headquarters on Erzébet Királnö (Queen Elizabeth), where he spends the night. The next day, he makes a brief appearance at the Swedish Legation, where he doles out money to his Hungarian assistants. He slips on the ice in front of the Swedish hospital. The hospital manager helps him up and walks him to his car. 'I'll be back from Debrecen in a week.' The Studebaker disappears on the road east, flanked by a Soviet motorcycle escort with sidecars.

— ◆ —

At the end of converging lines of hedges and fences, in the snowy village of Herrlisheim, across from an Alsatian inn, men of a US Infantry medical section lean against an ambulance that is well stocked with champagne bottles. They pass a bottle of schnapps, puffing their cigarettes. 'Geez, that's a sin,' says one, wiping his mouth.

'A mortal sin,' says another gravely. 'Fucked this broad right in the snowbank. Right in the goddamn snowbank. How do you like that?'

The combat surgeon enjoys and records these exchanges in his diary, but a part of him doubts the value of words. When blood comes spurting through a mass of torn clothes, muscles, bones, and subcutaneous tissues ripped away, forming a twisted, matted jungle, the word *anatomy* might seem incongruous.

Near dawn, after deafening firing with a rush of their artillery coming in overhead, as men keep materializing out of fog, white with snow, exhausted and matted with blood, he sees a wounded, profoundly happy shadow approaching the tent, whooping like a drunk in a Western saloon, flesh ripped from his thigh. The medics push him gently down to cut clothing away. He waves his M-1 rifle around. He won't let it go. Two years he carried that fucker around and cleaned it and drilled with it and marched with it, and today he got the Kraut right in the ring-sights and he squeezed down, and he killed the son of a bitch.

In the aid station, so many of them want to return to the front to be with their friends. Simultaneously, the wounded soldiers witness some token of humanity. They see that the medics want to keep them from harm, and they open up. Some soldiers are whimpering remnants on litters, terrified into a fetal position, incapable of anything except convulsive shivering.

Medics sponge with an aid packet, while a helper gently loosens the tourniquet to let the bleeding start just enough for recognition. The high-pressure arteries spurt first but they can hardly ever be located. The task then is to put in a suture and hope for occlusion. Hopefully the dressings will be enough to staunch small veins and capillaries.

Working without gloves and with no time to boil instruments, Brendan Phibbs somehow does pretty well with instruments carried in jars of sterilizing solutions. They work as a team. He ties sutures using two hemostats, while a helper holds a third. It's efficient. The surgeon has learned to inject a local anesthetic quickly, all through the wound. His irritability is a different matter when supplies of novocaine are down.

'Mind you, fifty bloody Tiger tanks tomorrow at dawn.' The supply officer has been arguing with the artillery commander and it looks like, this side of Paris, the artillery has just fifty rounds of ammunition.

A kind of delirium, a paralyzing fear insinuates itself among the soldiers. The terror is palpable. Twenty minutes of ammunition. You know that something is seriously wrong when you observe cooks in the mess truck, pots and pans flying, looking for a bazooka.

Fresh-falling, quieting snow. Shapes of glum men and guns. Muffled sounds, and that implacable logic. The men keep staring at each other. 'It's the fuckin' rear echelon, those bastards with their eight-hour days and their French whores and their black market …' A sergeant pounds his fists against the wall. 'Them fuckheads, them fuckheads, them cowardly lazy fuckheads! After all we've done, after all we've been through, after the way we beat those goddam Krauts!'

At the command post the new colonel is taking charge. They call him 'Charlie' or 'West Man'. He saved them all earlier, opposing an untimely suicide attack, defiantly hindering strict orders. Waiting for dawn, Phibbs recalls friends at home, safely crossing Grand Central, making their way to suburban homes. Children are asleep, teddy bears and dolls and games on the living-room floor.

As explosions rock the command post in the basement, 'Charlie' shouts orders. Those observing him are convinced the radios can't possibly function. 'Stop this goddam panic!' Amid frantic sounds and shell bursts, people are doubled over. Phibbs' kneecaps begin to twitch uncontrollably. The colonel slams the phone down, 'We're not retreating anywhere.'

— ◆ —

Buchenwald is a concentration camp situated near Weimar in central Germany. The camp opened in 1937 and, by now, almost 240,000 prisoners have been sent there. In early January, effective immediately, the Nazi authorities have decided to halve food rations to finish off all prisoners.

At the very bottom of a strict prison hierarchy are those known as *Muselmänner*, who have but a few days to live. Among those who are past caring, we find a pint-sized, blind French Resistance fighter. Arrested in Paris, he survived thirty brutal interrogation sessions. One of his five interrogators tossed him against the wall. At the end of each day, with a guiding hand in the back of his neck, Jacques was pushed down corridors and stairs, shoved into a van and driven back to prison. The next day, another interrogation session would begin. The Germans can't quite fathom how a blind person could be a Resistance leader.

When the train pulled out of the station in Paris, the French prisoners sang a rousing '*Marseillaise*'. The weather was freezing. Upon arrival, as they tumbled out of the wagons, a fellow inmate broke his wrist intercepting a rifle butt that was meant to finish off the blind laggard. Now they have locked up Jacques with demented and paralyzed people, crawling upon each other like worms.

— ◆ —

The first liberators arrive on horseback at midday on a snowy, but sunny Saturday. The Soviet troops discovered the Auschwitz camp almost by chance. The stench is beyond description, something like a monkey-house, more hallucination than reality. Inside the barbed wire, corpses are scattered everywhere, with unwieldy piles by the doors of the huts. There's little obvious difference between the dead and the living – haggard survivors with faces like hunted beasts.

The Red Army soldiers point to the stars on their caps, '*Germania Kaputt*' and '*Russki! Russki*'.

Huge eyes, 'SS?'

'*Nix SS, Hitler Kaputt!*'

The Russian soldiers say more help is coming, looking sideways, looking elsewhere. The *Häftlinge* have reached untouchable depths of degradation. '*Kasha, Kasha!*' they shout, imitating someone putting food in their mouth. They have tears in their eyes but can't even shed them.

'*Da*', perhaps three or four camps. The interference is frustrating. The signals operators look at one another. Majdanek times four? Ask them again.

Other units think the trouble can be subdued. More medical help, food, water, nurses, medical personnel. We need to requisition supplies from the surrounding villages and towns, and a liaison regiment to clear this up, and a film and photo unit. No, electricity's down. No, start with aerial views of the factories. There's no light inside the huts.

A Red Army colonel learns about the death camp from the commander of the 100th Division and makes his way to Auschwitz. What is he expected to do? This isn't just one camp, but vast compounds behind high-voltage barbed wire. He peeks into barracks that have been sprayed by machine-gun fire. He notices pools of frozen, glass-like blood and piles of corpses inside. He discovers successive sites.

The crematoria were not abandoned by the SS but dynamited. One was still intact on 26 January, just before Soviet troops reached Auschwitz. The flames over there? That's what's left of the thirty barracks of 'Canada II'. The warehouses of 'Canada I', here, were left alone. By the *Bahnrampe*, seven wagons are standing, full of male and female clothes, perhaps half a million pieces. His soldiers show him bags filled with hair and tell him there are 7 tons of hair – 7 tons?

Prisoners stumble behind him to act as witnesses. They mumble in fifty languages. There are mountains of suitcases, glasses, dental fixtures. Surrounded by other officers, the colonel now comes across eighty-odd children near an empty experiment room. The ache inside his head will never end. The Germans have taken the surgical tables with them and just about everything else, even tweezers.

The Red Army officer doesn't know where to begin. Who is going to clean this mess up? Should he assist the children first? We need the Polish Red Cross. Now!

— ◆ —

The wartime love letter discloses and bares. 'My Darling,' writes Clementine Churchill from 10 Downing Street, 'I was much relieved to get the signal you had reached Malta safely, flying with the blizzard on your tail.' She mentions the delectable little London house they visited together in Kensington. It's a brief letter, which ends on a high note: 'Seven inches of snow fell last night but it's much less cold – the radio announced this morning that coal distribution by Army lorries begins to-day! It didn't mention who thought of this.'

The prime minister has left London on 29 January 1945 in his luxurious, four-engine Skymaster, stopping in Malta on the first lap of his journey to Yalta. Traveling to 'the Riviera of Hades', as he calls it, Churchill finds solace in the presence of his daughter, Sarah. From Malta he sends Clementine a coded telegram for 'Mrs. Kent from Colonel Kent', 'Quite well again but spend most time in bed in *Orion*'s comfortable cabin. Miss you very much. The world is in a frightful state.'

In truth, Churchill has had a high temperature for several hours and cannot be transferred from the aircraft to the cruiser, HMS *Orion*. His physician, Lord Moran, is lost for an explanation.

Churchill considers this the closing phase of his life. Black velvet, eternal sleep is near. He will be carried to a better world. 'When it comes to dying, I shall not complain. I shall not meow.'

Although a careful planner with a keen eye for detail, Churchill is an inveterate optimist when it comes to risk and risk-taking. A long time ago, he had fired at Boers and they had captured the military train in which he was traveling, then he had escaped. During the First World War, he had surmounted the failure of the Dardanelles and, by a hair, avoided deadly artillery fire in the trenches. In Manhattan, he was struck by a car arriving from the right. He was taken to the Lennox Hill Hospital, where he developed pleurisy. Several times, engine trouble in an airplane had nearly ended his life. At the previous conference with Allied leaders in Teheran, he had struggled hard with pneumonia.

Looking out from HMS *Orion*'s deck into Valletta Harbor, the prime minister sees widespread destruction. Rusting hulks peek out of the water and twisted copper and zinc the color of oysters points to much aerial bombing. Not even the warm colors and brilliant sunshine can cheer him up. Churchill is aware that he needs to review vital maps, charts, and papers in Malta to prepare for the Big Three meeting in Yalta. However, an RAF York transport aircraft carrying staff members from the Foreign Office and War Cabinet has bypassed Malta in the fog and has been lost at sea along with the precious research papers. Churchill acutely feels the loss of life and vital documents.

Noticing the palette of warm colors slightly reminiscent of the Atlas Mountains, as he leans over the balustrade of HMS *Orion* Churchill cannot help but recount his implacable feud with Adolf Hitler. What would have happened if they had met in September 1932 in Munich? To trace the life of his forebear, John Churchill, 1st Duke of Marlborough, Churchill had crossed the Channel to see the scenes of past military victories. He had journeyed through Belgium and Holland and a friend of a friend had tried to introduce him to Hitler in the Bavarian capital. He had waited at his hotel, but Hitler never showed up, despite the pleas of the go-between. In any case, Hitler had asked, 'What part does Churchill play? Isn't he in the opposition, and no one pays attention to him, right?' 'And so are you', the go-between had replied.

Next, he had wanted to continue his journey to Venice for a holiday but then had been taken ill with paratyphoid fever. Two weeks in a sanatorium in Salzburg.

In late September, Churchill had returned to England to proceed with Marlborough's biography but then, walking in the grounds of Chartwell, he had collapsed. A recurrence of the paratyphoid. An ambulance had driven him to a nursing home in London. A severe hemorrhage from a paratyphoid ulcer. What if he had died that early fall and Hitler had been defeated the following year at the 1933 elections?

Churchill decides to write a long letter to Clementine, telling her he is looking forward to meeting Harry Hopkins that night. Towards the end of his letter, he expresses concern for German mothers: 'I must confess to you that my heart is saddened by the talks of the masses of German women and children flying along the roads everywhere in forty-mile-long columns to the West before the advancing Armies.' Churchill knows that there are 8 million ethnic Germans trapped in Russian territory:

> Tender Love my darling
> I miss you very much
> I am lonely amid this throng
> Your ever loving husband

> W

— ✦ —

Under heavy escort, USS *Quincy* is at long last expected to complete its 5,000-mile journey tomorrow. Tethered to their listening devices, the sonar men below deck were especially nervous, convinced the enemy knew of this presidential voyage. Heliograph messages kept warning of potential German U-boat gates.

A grand reception at Gibraltar. Surrounded by a phalanx of Secret Service men, including one exceptional swimmer, President Roosevelt retires early, sleeps late, and has breakfast with his daughter, Anna. In the evening, he watches a motion picture with aides and close friends.

The deep, steady roll of USS *Quincy* at times inflicts atrocious pain on the hips of President Roosevelt. Meanwhile, the Yalta research material and recommendations prepared by the State Department remain below deck. Lifting and falling easily in a head sea, *Quincy* begins a series of fast zig-zag maneuvers approaching the southern tip of the Iberian Peninsula.

Once inside the Mediterranean, *Quincy* makes radio contact with Tangier.

The mood on board noticeably lightens past the Strait of Gibraltar because of fewer U-boats in the Mediterranean. Lucky day. The mood is such that the staff spontaneously insist on another party for the president, because today – 30 January – is his birthday. In the small dining room, no fewer than four birthday cakes are presented to Roosevelt: one from his favorite Filipino chef, one from staff officers, another one from the warrant officers, and a fourth one from the crew, with an odd inscription engraved in icing. Is it the number '5', for a fifth term, or an odd question mark in the shape of lazy inverted 'S' that provokes hilarity?

Roosevelt decides he needs fresh air in the company of Anna. The president's wheelchair emerges along the gray silhouette of *Quincy* and sailors crowd the deck to gape and gawk. Anna instinctively looks for the gun mount that screens the wind, conscious of her father's sinus flare-ups. The tender moment of togetherness is captured on film.

— ◆ —

Mexico City is a bucolic haven of peace. Frida Kahlo sits at her easel, painting, taking a long look at a simple bouquet of magnolias, which she started a month earlier. The ivory-white flowers bloomed a fortnight earlier. Jacqueline Lambda held the splendid flower in front of her, slightly higher than her gaze, then she gave it to her daughter, Aube. The scent is dignified, overpowering. Frida Kahlo cannot take her eyes off her *trompe l'oeil* effect when she inserted an oversized cactus flower amid the creamy white petals. The short flight of female beauty and evanescent color harmony.

It's the next day. Frida Kahlo wakes up in her bed and catches a glimpse of herself in the mirror encased above the bed, a gift from her father. She loved her father. 'You don't need feet when you have wings,' he told her. She starts painting her face, her gift. Begin with sunshine.

She hears them distinctly just before dawn. Spider monkeys, hairless dogs, macaws, hens, an eagle, and a fawn. Sounds of chains rattling. The two parakeets are chirping, squawking. The animals are so loud across the patio of Casa Azul, and it's so early. If the Nazis could arrest Frida, they would immediately do it. Degenerate art!

— ✦ —

Svetlana Alliluyeva is three months pregnant and looking healthy. The father of the baby is Grigory Morozov, a student at the Moscow Institute of International Affairs. The two got married the previous year when she was 18. They just moved into the House on the Embankment, a block-wide apartment building on the banks of the Neva.

Svetlana Alliluyeva is vivacious, smart, and her English is excellent. She found out about her mother's suicide, for instance, from foreign magazines. So, it wasn't an ordinary death.

The pictures reveal her as the apple of her father's eye. Aged 16, Svetlana met the irresistible, 38-year-old Aleksei Kapler, the most famous screenwriter in the USSR. She was young and his love of risk excited her. What was Kapler thinking when he invited her to dance? Her bodyguard started sweating profusely, but what could he do when this Jew from the Moscow intelligentsia approached her? Rush between them and reach for his gun?

Kapler loved what he called the freedom within her and her bold judgments. She thought him the cleverest, kindest, most intelligent person on earth. They watched Greta Garbo's *Queen Christina* together and he bought her Hemingway's banned *For Whom the Bell Tolls*. When she telephoned him from her grandmother's apartment in the Kremlin, she called him 'Lyusa', and her grandmother thought she was talking to a girlfriend. But Stalin knew everything.

Kapler was a man of honor, perhaps that was the real scandal, and he could not be intimidated. He had written a cryptic article in *Pravda* about their relationship. Ostensibly a soldier's description of Stalingrad, the piece was in effect a love letter to Svetlana: 'My love, who knows whether this letter will reach you?' He describes watching snow falling outside the Kremlin walls and asks if she remembers their rendezvous at the Tretyakov Gallery.

'Your Kapler is a British spy!' Stalin said. Turning to her nanny, he said, 'Oh, she loves him …' Then Stalin slapped Svetlana across the face for the first time in her life.

It wasn't long before Kapler signed his confession. After a year in solitary confinement, he was deported to Vorkuta. Deep inside her, however, Svetlana knows that they will be reunited.

— ✦ —

What would have happened if, late in 1944, a US reconnaissance pilot by the name of Lieutenant Rudolf Shaw had not met with engine trouble and decided to parachute to safety? Local Viet Minh units had been the first to reach him, while French patrols were sent to locate him. The Viet Minh did not speak a word of English, which was unnerving.

Wearing a threadbare and patched Kuomintang military uniform, with thin canvas shoes full of holes, Ho Chi Minh had introduced himself in colloquial English. It would later be said that this man had an extraordinary gift to immediately establish relationships with his interlocutors, whether they were ministers or peasants. Some have even called him a dangerous comedian.

Ho had next offered to accompany the American flyer back to the Kunming base in China. During the arduous trek by night, Ho Chi Minh had enquired about the possibility of obtaining a radio, as well as arms and medicine.

When instructing his comrades in arms, Ho frequently insisted on waiting for the right moment (*tho co* or *co hoi*), yet it was tough to keep up with the rapidly changing situation. The northern region was suffering from rampant famine. The Japanese refused to open state granaries or to allow rice shipments from the fertile Mekong Delta to the north. In the cities, rich bourgeois people were trading their jewelry, while peasants had started to eat roots, weeds, and even the bark of trees. On the ideological front, the French imperialist wolf is about to devour the Japanese fascist hyena.

Ho looks like a frail peasant with silver hair. In a world of political survivors, he is in a league of his own. When he left his country in 1911, together with a few hundred other young Vietnamese, little did he know that he would spend thirty years dodging security forces in half a dozen countries. In 1914, he had escaped to London, working as a dishwasher and assistant pastry hand in a hotel. Back in France, he had made an appearance at the Paris Peace Conference.

In the 1920s, he had learned the techniques of clandestine work and revolutionary leadership in Moscow. When Stalin had decided on the 'united front strategy' and purged the ranks of the Comintern, Ho Chi Minh was out of reach in Canton, Shanghai, and Hong Kong.

Back in Moscow in the late thirties, Ho had kept a low profile. He had crossed back into Vietnam in February 1941. Denounced and arrested, he had languished in eighteen different prisons in the Guangxi province for two years. At Kunming, the underground fighters hesitate to open a couture shop close to the US Embassy. Ho suggests that they open *Dong Zuong caphe*, Café Indochine. The idea is to connect with OSS operatives.

February

Airplanes transporting Churchill and Franklin D. Roosevelt (FDR) begin a pre-approved maneuver before landing at Saki Airbase. On his armored train, Stalin peruses Beria's report on Yalta security measures. In liberated Auschwitz, Polish Red Cross nurses carry two feather-light Italian sisters, feeding them kasha by the spoon.

It is still dark on Corregidor in the Philippines and one can hear fierce machine-gun fire in the surrounding area. A group of captive American nurses watch a dark silhouette jump off a tank. Does he speak English?

In East Prussia, a young Red Army captain by the name of Alexander Solzhenitsyn is ordered to surrender his revolver. This must be a mistake.

On the fifth day of battle at Iwo Jima island, Marines raise a flag on Mount Suribachi. In Paris, Picasso begins an oversized painting that will sum up the entire war, something as meaningful as *Guernica*. After six long years of separation, Simone de Beauvoir is reunited with her sister in Lisbon and the two talk until dawn, then fall asleep.

US President Franklin D. Roosevelt and British Prime Minister Winston Churchill with their daughters, Anna Boettiger and Sarah Churchill, aboard the heavy cruiser USS *Quincy* (CA-71) in Malta before the Yalta Conference, 2 February 1945. (FDR Presidential Library & Museum photo 48-22 3659)

It's time to head to the airport. The exodus from Malta begins at 11.30 p.m. with a flotilla of RAF Yorks and Spitfires, as well as Lockheed Lightnings and C-54s. They are taking off at ten-minute intervals, all observing radio silence. The night sky is dusted with winter stars. The president's private airplane, named 'The Sacred Cow' because it is constantly surrounded by guards, takes off at 3.30 a.m. By that time, the frail old man is long asleep. One by one, the planes head toward Crete, where they make a 90-degree turn toward the Aegean Sea and the Dardanelles – and then, beyond, to the Black Sea.

Approaching Soviet territory, the Western Allies must make a prearranged identification maneuver, before entering a 20-mile-wide corridor and making a right turn to land on the icy Saki Airbase. The president's airplane lands at Saki on 3 February at 12.10 p.m. local time. He waits for Churchill's plane to stop next to his. Roosevelt is lowered in an elevator specially designed by the Douglas Aircraft Company and is carried to a Lend–Lease Jeep. Churchill lights up another 8in cigar. He follows Roosevelt's Jeep on foot – an undignified scene to his doctor, Lord Moran, to whom Churchill resembles an Indian attendant accompanying Queen Victoria's phaeton.

Roosevelt and Churchill review the Soviet Guard of Honor and then the Red Army band plays the Soviet, British, and American national anthems. FDR tells Vyacheslav Molotov that the 'Star Spangled Banner' is rendered beautifully. The latter nods without turning his head.

The reception afterwards is a memorable affair. Are we at war? The Russians have installed three refreshment tents. Rows of vodka, brandy and champagne bottles stand to attention. The display for foreign dignitaries is second to none. Dishes of caviar, salmon, smoked sturgeon, white and black bread, butter, cheese, soft boiled eggs: all of this speaks wonders about Russian hospitality. Lavish samovars and lovely glasses of tea with lemon and sugar.

Vyacheslav Molotov, the USSR's Foreign Commissar, is the first to greet the American president. He has a very low opinion of Roosevelt, regarding him as an imperialist who would grab anyone by the throat. It's puzzling to him that a paralyzed man can become President of the United States, and for *three* terms! What a rascal you had to be! Then again, Americans are notoriously thick-skinned and only concerned with their pocketbooks.

Shaking Molotov's hand, Roosevelt enquires about Stalin. This polite query is met with a formal, if evasive, answer. Molotov tells the president that regrettably he doesn't know Marshal Stalin's whereabouts. Known as 'Mr Nyet' in diplomatic circles, Molotov is an accomplished liar. In fact, he has been in constant touch with Stalin at the Yusupov Palace and has one more phone call to make to inform the boss that Churchill and Roosevelt have come with their daughters, as has Ambassador Harriman.

As the dignitaries climb into black limousines, a weary Churchill dreads the drive to a place reputedly good for typhus and deadly on lice. He muses: we had the world at our feet. We seemed to be friends. We had 25 million men marching under our orders on land and sea, day and night.

The curves on the road are short and sharp. With no retaining wall, it sometimes juts out over the abyss. Every hundred yards, shivering Russian soldiers, most of them women, stand to attention. Shouldering tommy guns, they salute firmly as the Packards and Zils drive past on winding, war-torn roads.

Churchill fears the US President will aim for special deals with Stalin at Europe's expense. The British Prime Minister

Vyacheslav Molotov (center) at the Yalta Conference. (NARA NAID: 204998861 (US Air Force Number 70193AC))

feels strangely detached. The only ray of light is that after the war he will be one of the historians – *My War and Peace* – Churchill is keen to use his unrivalled access to Cabinet papers, and he needs to give his family financial security. Words, after all, are the only things that last forever.

— ◆ —

His low-pitched voice, almost halting, is known to everybody in the USSR. They call him 'Koba' or 'Khozyan'. His face is everywhere on gigantic posters and banners, sometimes next to Marx and Lenin. Up close, his face is pockmarked and yellow. His broken teeth are hard to ignore. He usually holds a pipe and is at his most dangerous and unpredictable when it is unlit. Stalin is also difficult to read when his pudgy fingers hold American cigarettes or when his sinister tiger's eyes close.

The train station swarms with NKVD officers. Groups of anti-aircraft gunners are waiting on their freezing flatcars. Walking next to Nicolai Vlasik, his chief bodyguard, Stalin enters the famous green 83-ton Pullman carriage. The bulletproof saloon with a reinforced concrete floor has every amenity, including a conference room with a glass table to accommodate the closest entourage.

Stalin's desk is stacked with files and dispatches from the Stavka. Right now, Stalin is studying maps showing planned advances on German territory. *Turn forces north to Pomerania.* At Yalta, Stalin wants to discuss military questions first. They need to grasp that Russia has paid the highest price in blood and will now set its price for peace. America provided Dodge trucks, but we paid in blood.

Vlasik usually ranks reports by order of relevance. Secret Police Chief Lavrentiy Beria's report is predictably on top, and the details are mind-numbing: some 244 airplanes protect the airspace above the Crimea and some 300 anti-aircraft batteries are stationed at Yalta. The special 'Vch' high-frequency tele-phone line is in place, as well as an automatic telephone of twenty numbers to call Moscow, the Stavka and fronts, all towns, and it can be extended to fifty if need be. The palaces are defended by 160 fighter planes and a plethora of anti-aircraft guns. Two circles of guards by day and three by night have been added to the 620 bodyguards.

At the Livadia Palace, where Stalin is staying, workers have constructed a bomb and gas shelter with a concrete ceiling 2m thick with a 1m-deep sand cover capable of withstanding a direct hit. As an extra precaution, the five districts surround-ing Yalta have been purged of suspicious elements: 74,000 have been checked and 835 arrested. What is more, every palace is bugged.

At the Yalta Conference, Prime Minister Winston S. Churchill, President Franklin D. Roosevelt, and Premier Joseph Stalin make final plans for the defeat of Germany. (NARA NAID: 531340 Local ID: 111-SC-260486)

— ◆ —

The stout Polish nurses are swearing under their breath as they try to sort this mess out. It's the Devil's work. They are nursing skeletons back to life, one spoon of *kasha* at a time. '*Kasha, khorosha*'. Two sisters look at one another in disbelief. Lea Gattegno and her sister Virginia wonder whether they are the only survivors of their Rhodes community. At night, Lea lies on her bunk bed, hallucinating. A child's voice in the dark, 'Mother, water – mother, water', a soft voice. Thick, hideous darkness. She hears the commotion outside. Someone is lifting her gently. A soldier puts Lea on the back of a truck. Lea catches a glimpse of parallel railway lines. The truck drives over a bridge and under a gate into another camp. She is spoon-fed minuscule quantities of *kasha*, no bigger than her little finger. '*Kasha khorosha*', the sisters joke.

— ◆ —

They form the largest group of captive army and navy nurses in US history. Thin and gaunt, there are sixty-five of them still alive at the Santo Tomas Internment Camp and Los Baños Prison Camp on Corregidor Island in the Philippines. For three years, they survived on 500 calories a day, caring for a ragtag group of mangled men and emaciated children.

In the early hours of 3 February, the nurses hear machine-gun fire nearby, followed by the sound of iron toppling to the ground. The ominous shadow of a tank rolls up and stops in front of the main building. Two men in uniform climb out and look up at the windows. 'Hello, folks!'

Screaming and shouting, tears rolling down, most internees drop to their knees while a throng rushes outside to surround the tanks. They try to make sense of the small, painted American flags. In the melee, nearly everyone wants to touch the liberators. The men look like giants. 'My lands, how come you fellows are so big!?' The nicknames inscribed on the barrels are endearing: 'BATTLIN' BASIC', 'GEORGIA PEACH', 'KLANKING KOFFIN'.

Amid searchlights, a lone voice is heard singing:

God bless A–mer–i–ca …

Other voices instantly join in:

… Land that I love.
Stand beside her,
And guide her,
Through the night
With the light
From above.

— ◆ —

Arrest is instantaneous. In a few minutes, the first part of Alexander Solzhenitsyn's life will be a thing of the past. On 9 February, SMERSH (Death to Spies!) Red Army counter-intelligence officers from the counter-espionage service will pin a '10-ruble bill' on him, as the expression goes, and ship him to a labor camp in Siberia. If he co-operates, it will be eight years.

The twice-decorated captain is stationed just east of Königsberg. Days earlier, his battalion was attacked, and, under heavy rifle fire, he discovered that sensation of weightlessness, that moment when scenes from your past rush through your head.

Solzhenitsyn grew up without a father and must carve a path for himself in life. The young man by no means sees himself as a writer. He is a dedicated Komsomol Youth, a double-major student in engineering and mathematics at the University of Moscow, and the proud recipient of the prestigious Stalin Prize.

At the outset of the Great Patriotic War, he was rejected at the recruiting station. The memory still sears.

He finds work with rear units, where old Cossacks mock him mercilessly as he corrals horses and mucks out manure from stalls. The greenhorn doesn't know the front from the rear of a horse. Be that as it may, Solzhenitsyn learns to ride, and from there worms his way into artillery school. Like every recruit, he is licked into submission and endures severe punishments for the most trivial offenses.

Lately, Solzhenitsyn has been complaining to his dearest friend Lydia Ezherets – Lida to her friends – about not receiving letters from their penpal, Nikolai Vitkevich. Similarly, Nikolai – Koka to his friends – has written to Lydia, mentioning Solzhenitsyn's odd silence.

Lydia comes from an educated and prominent Jewish family. She is a gentle and utterly selfless girl. Solzhenitsyn tries sending Nikolai a letter by way of Lydia and somehow that letter reaches its destination. In their correspondence, the two men agree on grand plans for the post-war order and gently mock Stalin, nicknaming him the diminutive '*Balabos*', Yiddish for 'Master of the House'.

On the day of his arrest, Solzhenitsyn receives a message from Brigade Headquarters telling him to report at once to Brigadier General Travkin. As he enters the brigadier's office, Travkin orders him to hand over his revolver. His commanding officer winds the leather strap slowly round the butt and places it in his drawer. As it closes, two officers from SMERSH step forward. 'You are under arrest,' they say.

Strange as this may seem, the normally attentive and perceptive Solzhenitsyn has never noticed people disappearing. His meek, incredulous 'Me? What for?' will be repeated millions of times across the Eurasian landmass. The SMERSH officers rip the epaulets from his shoulders. They remove the star from his cap and belt. They confiscate his map case.

Over time, Solzhenitsyn will carry the destiny of Russia on his shoulders, but right now he is a traitor, a counter-revolutionary, a wrecker. They are scared they'll be linked to this pariah, this spy. As he is led out, Travkin barks, 'Solzhenitsyn, come back here!'

Other officers in the brigade shield their eyes in a corner of the tent. Deafening silence. Indicating where the danger has come from, he asks, 'Have you a friend on the First Ukrainian Front?'

The political officers shout, 'That's against regulations! You have no right!' They don't hesitate to shout, even at a general.

Ignoring them, Travkin gets to his feet and shakes Solzhen-itsyn's hand. 'I wish you happiness, Captain.'

— ◆ —

From the air, the tiny pinpoint of lava looks like a pork chop floating in the Pacific. Iwo Jima is only 5 miles long. Located 640 miles south of Tokyo Bay, the small speck has two finished airfields and a third which is partially completed. The rocky island is honeycombed with heavy Japanese fortifications and ever-deeper bunkers. At its southern tip, you can see Mount Suribachi, which is only 500ft high.

US forces want this island to eliminate the threat of Japanese fighters intercepting US Air Force aircraft. They also want it for their medium bombers, as a center for air–sea rescue for ditched crews, and to serve damaged B-29s returning from bombing runs on the Japanese mainland.

The whole place reeks of sulphur. The rocky canyons and volcanic ash terrain is a nightmare to waves of amphibious marine forces. Japanese defensive forces remain stubbornly in their well-fortified dugouts. Marines must discover veiled cave entrances and collapse them with flamethrowers. The Japanese fight with immense bravery.

On 23 February, amid deafening artillery fire and constant machine-gun rattle, a small flag is raised on the crest of Mount Suribachi. The hillsides are so steep that a broad assault must be rejected in favor of a small assault patrol. Marines on the island wave and cheer in the direction of the flag. US Navy vessels blow their horns. The uproar is reminiscent of a reaction to a touchdown. A cameraman at the top of Mount Suribachi catches the historic moment on film, then dives down the length of the crater to escape grenade attacks. His camera breaks, but the film miraculously survives.

The Americans are not aware that before the landings, Japanese Commander Tadamichi Kuribayashi officially prohibited heroic *bansai* attacks, which he thought would ultimately be less effective than holding on to hidden, defensive positions. The assault group on top of Mount Suribachi could easily have been overwhelmed. Even though Japanese forces know they are surrounded and doomed, their goal is to inflict horrendous casualty rates.

The historic moment raises the mood of Secretary of the Navy James Forrestal, watching from the command ship at Iwo Jima. Standing next to General Holland Smith, he expresses the wish to inspect the beach in person. After a few hesitations, he is put aboard a landing craft. When they arrive on shore, they see a second, much larger Stars and Stripes unfurling at the crest of Mont Suribachi. Forrestal is ecstatic. 'Holland,' he says, 'the raising of that flag means a Marine Corps for the next 500 years.'

Hours before, a colonel by the name of Johnson ordered a ship's flag, measuring 8 × 4½ft, to replace the first. At 54 × 28in, the first flag was barely visible in the distance.

Escorted by two soldiers, a near-sighted civilian photographer by the name of Jack Rosenthal had climbed to the summit. As the marines attached the new flag to a heavy metal pipe, he aimed his camera. The overcast noonday light gave

US Marines raising the flag on Iwo Jima. (NARA NAID: 520748 Photograph 80-G-413988)

The hand of a Japanese soldier killed by a bomb blast. (NARA NAID: 520735 Photograph 80-G-412532)

sculptural depth to the six soldiers as they crouched forward and looked up. A gust of wind imparted a sense of action.

The spontaneous event seems timeless: a simple means to defeat the enemy and achieve national goals in the Pacific. There are also cameramen who catch the scene on film – these take time to develop, but the AP transfers the picture by wire. It is splashed on the front pages of US newspapers two days later. For publicity and patriotic reasons, Iwo Jima is larger than life.

— ◆ —

Dazed by the horrific revelations seeping out of Germany, Picasso begins his work on *The Charnel House*, his largest canvas since *Guernica*. He tones down colors, reducing the loose scheme to strict grisaille. At the bottom of the loose pyramidal composition, the piled-up cadavers look like refuse, human limbs twisting in pain stacked up in a heap: a father, a mother, and a baby lying backwards. Everything is true and everything is false. The mother's milk flows between the baby's fingers, or is it blood that feeds the base of this jungle of lines? In the upper part of the scene, a table and utensils insert a note of serenity. War has a way of crashing open the door of domestic bliss.

This is his moment of truth. Picasso's friend Cocteau visits the artist's studio, and the pair talk about the necessity of going fast to preserve freshness, the initial impulse.

— ◆ —

Simone de Beauvoir leaves Paris by train on the evening of 27 February. She hasn't traveled abroad in six years and hasn't seen Spain in fifteen. She starts reading *Brighton Rock* by Graham Greene, falling asleep just before dawn. When she wakes up at the last stop, the border town of Hendaye, the sky is an infinite blue.

Crossing a border is still a rare privilege. All passengers have to step off. Together with an old man, she is the only person to continue to Madrid. As the Customs officials check her papers, Simone de Beauvoir notices a woman along the road selling oranges, bananas, and chocolate, and this just 10 yards or so from the French border. Why was this abundance kept from the French?

Back on the train, the old man tells her that women seeing her walk with her suitcase had commented, 'She is a poor lady. She can't afford silk stockings.' And it's true, on the road to Madrid, women are laughing and wearing silk stockings. In Madrid, the abundance in the shops along the main thorough-fares makes her quite dizzy. Silk, wool, leather, olives, cakes, *gambas*, fried eggs, chocolate with cream, dried raisins – she feels like eating and walking, walking and eating. Madrid is sparkling under the sun.

She finds herself at the Prado the next day to admire paintings by Greco and Goya, yet instead of feeling elated and uplifted she feels sluggish, as though a thick fatigue is enveloping her body. She visits the University of Madrid campus, which is being rebuilt, and this somehow reminds her of destroyed parts of Normandy. One can see snowcapped mountains in the distance.

The reality of Franco's Spain catches up with her at long last. Policemen and soldiers are loitering on every corner. The procession of priests and children are clad in black and wearing crosses, walking next to well-fed bourgeois on the Gran Via. They probably wished for a German victory.

As she travels to villages north of Madrid, she comes across sordid neighborhoods where people are hungry. She takes a closer look at the prices in the marketplaces and understands why no one is smiling. Women wash rags on their doorsteps.

Saturn Devouring his Son by Francisco de Goya. (Prado Museum, Wikimedia Commons)

The villages have neither water nor sewers. The hard misery can be read on the faces. Madrid is but a façade. Only the people in train stations and in the capital city could afford the luxury.

On the train platform in Lisbon, de Beauvoir is reunited with her sister. The two talk in the streets, in the restaurant, at her apartment, until de Beauvoir all but faints with fatigue. As with Madrid, the lavishness in shops seems to belong to another age. Her sister asks, 'What are these galoshes you are wearing?'

Since the French Institute is generously funding de Beauvoir's conference tour, the two sisters go shopping together.

The French Institute also lends them a car and they tour the Algarve and admire the coastline, where cliffs drop abruptly into the ocean. They walk in gardens flowered with mimosas and enter small churches, where strange objects in wood, fabric, hair, and wax are treated as though they were relics from Christ and the saints.

It dawns on de Beauvoir that Portugal had granted all its sympathies to Germany during the war, but with Hitler now defeated, a rapprochement with France became essential. Hence the paid-for lecture tour.

The public who come to listen to de Beauvoir are partly idle, partly snobbish, and still quite enamored of Fascism. As de Beauvoir relays information about camps, executions, and torture, the listeners remain icy. Finally, the consular officer gets to his feet. 'Well,' he says, 'thank you for telling us things about which we were completely ignorant.' He makes sure to emphasize those last words.

March

Quick-thinking Yanks seize a bridge at Remagen over the Rhine, at once a remarkable feat and a stroke of luck. Women's Day, on 8 March, is a widely celebrated egalitarian symbol in the USSR. A feverish, semi-conscious Dutch teenager falls from her bunk bed at the Bergen-Belsen Camp. She spent a year recording her hopes and aspirations in a diary while in hiding in Amsterdam.

In the Arizona Desert, a 'Nazi' prisoner of war walks up to an African American nurse to declare his love. Binoculars in hand, Colonel Hiromichi Yahara gazes calmly at the Okinawa shoreline. His revised *bushidō* war doctrine will soon be tested.

Dr Alfred Kinsey gives numerous lectures to seek the special groups for his research on sexual behavior. Between Bordeaux and Paris, Monsieur le Baron de Rothschild is speed crazy. A new life in the countryside is on the cards.

Roaming through Greater Frankfurt in a Jeep, photographer Margaret Bourke-White is stopped by an old man in rags telling her the horse he is leading is a military horse. Where should he take it?

On 27 March, the last two V-2 rockets hit London. It's the final salvo of a terrifying missile campaign against the city. Betty Jean Jennings repeatedly turns down offers to become a math teacher. Instead, she makes her way to Philadelphia to work on a classified 'computer' project.

It is 8 March and 3.50 p.m. Across the Rhine, at Remagen, German engineers are preparing the bridge for demolition. But traffic coming from the west bank creates delays. The order is to blow up the bridge at 4 p.m., but retreating German units keep pulling over the bridge. American troops appear on the Rhine. Twenty-millimeter ack-ack guns guarding the bridge are firing away.

After a hurried meeting, American tanks begin pounding enemy gun emplacements on the other side and a first group of doughboys start racing over the bridge. Dynamite left by the Germans to destroy the bridge begins to explode. American engineers cut all the wires they find, and soon an avalanche of tanks and men roll over the bridge. For seven hours, one battalion of armored infantry holds the bridge alone.

The first men of the US Army cross Remagen Bridge. (NARA NAID: 531252 RG 111)

— ◆ —

'Look at the laundresses …' is a frequent scornful remark. Another one is 'Do they ever fight?' When they hear this, they feel hurt. Some women cry or complain to Valentina, the political commissar. 'You're doing your duty', is the response. The young women sometimes improvise a little dancing and singing among themselves, letting the men approach, only to spurn them. The whole evening by themselves. The soldiers finally plead, 'just because of one remark?' Too late now.

On this day – 8 March, Women's Day, a whopping egalitarian symbol in the Soviet Empire – a group of laundresses prepares to celebrate. They light a fire and gather a handful of sweets. At that moment, two wounded German soldiers dragging a machine gun emerge from the woods. The laundresses surround them to make them prisoners. Valentina, the political commissar, writes a report that on 8 March they captured two Germans. The next day, at a meeting with commanders, where the good news is shared that the war is almost over, everyone applauds.

Valentina finds out that her group of women is to be awarded two medals. Two awards? She is indignant. Her girls shouldn't have to go home empty-handed. She speaks up, saying that many laundresses have ruptures and eczema on their hands, that they work more than trucks, more than tractors. She is then asked to present more award-worthy laundresses by the next day.

That night, she works with her own commander on a long list to award more medals for laundresses. How do you define the activities of those who go through the war with a tub? What is award-worthy material when you look for a cottage and no mention of any washing machine? The laundresses carry cauldrons and pails. They scrounge for firewood, then they stoke the stoves. They do most of the strenuous work by hand. Heaps and heaps of heavy, padded jackets, black from old blood and heavy during the winter; army shirts with a big hole in the chest; ripped pants missing legs; underwear full of lice. White camouflage clothing all bloody, no longer white. You wash them with tears and rinse them with tears. Yet everything in due time, if you are still standing, inexplicably becomes a black-red heap. You feel nauseated. Blood and lice. There is always a shortage of soap. Most field bath-and-laundry units instead rely on ashes thrown in the cauldrons.

To complain would be dangerously unpatriotic. 'K' soap causes eczema and makes nails fall off. Many girls will receive medals 'For Valor', 'For Military Services', and one laundress is awarded 'The Order of the Red Star'. She never leaves the tub. When everyone is falling or sliding sideways with exhaustion, she keeps going. She's an older woman whose entire family has been killed.

— ✦ —

On 12 March, half-unconscious from fever, an adolescent girl rolls off her bunk bed in Bergen-Belsen. She falls lifeless from her bunk to the floor. On her thirteenth birthday, her father gave her a diary with a key, just before moving the family into a hiding place. For over a year, she kept a diary, while whispering and sitting still during the day.

Anne Frank was such a lively spirit that her diary does not speak of suffering. In most entries she simply shares hopes and fears with 'Kitty', the name of her diary. Every so often, Anne stuck a photograph of herself in her diary and commented on the picture: 'This is a photograph of me as I wish I looked all the time. Then I might still have a chance of getting to Hollywood. But at present, I'm afraid, I usually look quite different.' In an April 1944 entry, she wrote, 'I want to go on living even after my death! And therefore, I am grateful

The last known photograph of Anne Frank taken in May 1942 at a passport photo shoot. (Photo collection Anne Frank House, Amsterdam. Public Domain Work)

to God for giving me this gift, this possibility of developing myself and of writing, of expressing all that is in me.'

— ✦ —

At Camp Florence in the Arizona Desert, Frederick Albert is a German prisoner of war. The Germans are allowed out of camp to work in the cotton fields. The POWs are often struck at how violently Jim Crow laws are enforced. Frederick Albert is happy to work in the kitchen, where he is allowed to wear lightweight clothing and where he can catch jazz music on the radio. He frequently likes to take a glimpse into the dining area. He spots a beautiful, tall black woman.

Elinor Powell is a black American nurse in the US military. She is striking at 6ft, with regal posture. Frederick finds it hard to focus on his kitchen duties. Walking past several POW waiters, he looks her in the eyes and speaks with a German accent, 'You should bear my name. I'm the man who is going to marry you.' Maybe he wanted to say, 'You should hear my name' or 'You should bear my children'. It's a love story.

— ✦ —

Spring in its agonizing colorful plumpness is about to descend on Okinawa. The Americans will come at around cherry blossom time. Standing atop Mount Shuri at the southern end of the island, Colonel Hiromichi Yahara, binoculars in hands, gazes calmly over adjacent hills toward the Kadena coastline to the west. While on a map the island looks like the tiniest dot, it is much larger than anyone can imagine, some 120km north to the south and between 8 and 20km east to west. The time has come. At long last, Yahara feels the inner thrill of crossing swords with the enemy. He is known for his preternatural calm and detachment.

It will be the last great battle waged by the Imperial Japanese Army. An important task of any commanding officer is to predict *when* and *where* the enemy will appear on the horizon. Taking away the element of surprise is half the work. The other one, as Yahara sees it, is modifying age-old *banzai* tactics, and he did just that. Instead of charging ceaselessly, Japanese troops will now wait in their caves behind camouflaged fortifications.

At 42, Colonel Yahara is at the peak of his career. His lifelong project has been to strip away the *bushidō* myth of frontal attacks: the notion that the Japanese spirit is mightier than aerial bombs and naval gunfire. A frantic bayonet attack, grenades flying, is never the adequate response. Anyone who has even come close to US firepower from enemy-controlled skies and US Navy vessels knows this. The vaunted offensive spirit is suicidal. The only way to beat the Americans is through a war of attrition.

Colonel Yahara has ordered the building of many underground caves, methodically inspecting them. The aim now is for gunners to wait in their emplacements, avoiding giving away their positions prematurely, even when the massed armada is yards away. Let them radio back 'Where's the enemy?' In his heart, Yahara knows that he will be blamed for any setback. Months before, his best troops were taken out and put on troopships to the Philippines. He also knows that the promised air force and 'additional large units' will never materialize. The odds are what they are. The ground-fighting strength ratio will probably be 10 to 1, and with the massive earth-rending artillery much higher still. Americans own the skies.

What Colonel Yahara fears most is a change of tactics: a resurgence of the old line of reasoning in the heat of battle. His superior, Major General Cho, is a fire-eater, a boastful idiot. Sooner or later, steaming with enthusiasm, Cho will fall back on patented winning tactics. He will inevitably order not one but several self-annihilation assaults, each probably costing 5,000 lives. In response, Yahara will plead for more caution, for more time. Inevitably, Cho will modify his gambit, insisting on infiltrating the hard-nosed bastards and their machines, adding a swarm of suicide boats to intercept American transports. Sooner or later, maybe by the end of next month, after some desultory speech, Cho will take his own life.

— ✦ —

What price statistical glory! Dr Alfred Kinsey is on yet another grand tour of America, this time dividing his time between Chicago and New York, giving himself six weeks in these two cities to find more raw material for his study. His home base is Indiana University, a bedrock state of traditional values and conservative attitudes towards marriage. The Rockefeller Foundation overcame its reticence and funded his research on sexual behaviors, a landscape dappled with ignorance, a plethora of outdated laws, and as many interlocking religious prohibitions.

Kinsey invited his wife, Clara McMillen, to join him in New York. Among many others, Dr Kinsey has given lectures to five psychiatric groups, which have provided the histories of 150 psychiatrists. His total is now over 7,500 histories. In a world of euphemisms, slight winks, wry metaphors, and innuendos, Dr Kinsey's workload is crushing. With Clara and a handful of research associates, he wants to expand honest descriptions of sex beyond a single standard of sexual behavior. He is at heart a social reformer rather than a scrupulous statistician. Indeed, he rejected random sampling, simply because of the high number of refusals to participate in such a study. His focus is exploring intimate matters through frank interviews within special populations, be they prisoners or homosexuals. The key is inspiring confidence. There is a fine line, an elegant space, between voyeurism and sexual research, but someone has to do it, right? There will be a backlash for his reckless methodology and findings.

Dr Kinsey is a charismatic speaker. His bow tie is de rigueur. The resonant voice, the enthusiasm and tempo, the mastery of the topic is remarkable. One might say it's a distasteful task, mentioning words such as 'penis' and 'orgasm' repeatedly. He stands on the podium of an amphitheater, with a wall-length blackboard behind him. He looks into the eyes of his audience, feeling the adrenaline rush. What is the average? How many times?

He starts with one orgasm a month, then, the curve slowly rising, every three weeks, two weeks, a week, and then a pause, arms rising, twenty-five, thirty times a week, for twenty-five years. He stirs up profound astonishment, everyone in the audience thinking hard. A current of genuine surprise feeds the talk throughout. Time is banished, as Kinsey choreographs scientific jargon with rare, touching anecdotes. After every speech, curious or intrigued minds, electrified and exhilarated spirits approach him. Dr Kinsey unfailingly invites them to a bar near his hotel. He listens and talks until dawn about marital troubles, collecting names of potential correspondents.

In his quest to uncover sexual behavior throughout the ages, Dr Kinsey collects books of erotica. And he always welcomes sexual data from soldiers abroad. Ever so slowly, letters arrive from war-ravaged Europe, where the ease of sex for a pack of cigarettes is apparent. For instance, a GI tells him that 'the French fuck with their mouth and fight with their feet'. For the rest of his life, Kinsey will mistakenly believe that Europe is a haven of sexual liberation.

Every breakthrough leads to another problem in search of a solution, let's say, a new working hypothesis. In Chicago, a mother had condemned Kinsey for revealing that many girls were not ignorant of sex. What are the implications now?

At Howard University, an all-black college created to balance the preponderance of poor black Americans, Kinsey felt hostility to his methodology and storytelling. He is challenged for being a *white* man collecting black histories for a *white* book. His audience also rejects the binary opposition between white and black. If you intend to dismantle the sheep-and-goats dichotomy to instead narrate an array of practices, why rehearse this old story? After a great deal of defiance, some people in this educated audience agree to participate in the study.

— ◆ —

Monsieur le Baron likes to listen to old *vignerons* telling him that the year does not begin on 1 January, it begins with St Vincent in September. He has heard the story many times. They are shy and yet also happy to talk. They sit at the edge of their chair, cap in hand, in his office. All Saints', on 1 November, when the earth is asleep and the trees are bare, is for pruning, forever pruning. December is for muck spreading. In January, the women gather the brown bits fallen from the pruning to make sweet-scented fire and for grilling steaks. February is men's work again, with all the rows of stakes that need to be repaired. March? Raking up the dead leaves.

He had spent most of the war with the Free French in London. As a liaison officer with the Second British Army in liberated Paris, Baron Philippe had only two days' leave, yet he also wanted to find out about new beginnings for himself. He yearned to see what had happened to his property, the depredations, the thefts, whether or not his vines could still produce good wine. Apparently, there was still some sporadic fighting down there. Château Mouton had become the headquarters of the French Forces of the Interior (FFI). He had asked his daughter, Phillipine, if he should return. 'Only don't stay away so long this time, papa.'

Still in a beret and combat uniform, he had raced south in his Jeep, hardly noticing the burnt trucks and the bodies on his way to the south-west. Bordeaux was still intact, if dreary. Medoc itself was a sorry sight, a mass of ruined fields and empty houses. Closer to Mouton, the telegraph poles were down. A lot of debris would have to be cleared away – removing wires, repairing roads.

He had stopped outside his gate, some civilians giving him a salute, wearing the FFI red armband. Yes, the vines had been preserved. But he was rebuffed when he claimed back his château. 'It's confiscated,' came the haughty reply. Monsieur le Baron did not elaborate on having fought with the Free French. He pointed to his coat of arms over there. Is my portrait still in the living room? The new owner asks for two days to vacate, and then leaves with the furniture, stealing everything in sight.

This, then, is *almost* the end of the war. You have to take the rough with the smooth. Maybe the German prisoners of war could be employed in the vineyards and build a new road. When Wehrmacht troops had entered Paris in June 1940, Baron Philippe was recovering from a skiing accident. He fled to Casablanca and Vichy policemen arrested him. After close to a year of imprisonment and countless rounds of interrogation, he had escaped to London to join de Gaulle's resistance movement.

Predictably, both the Vichy regime and the occupying forces had competed to occupy the grand family mansions in central Paris. Yet the family had a special place in French hearts. French civil servants tried hard to block the legal looting. It was a special family, not defined by wealth alone: how the assets were privately held; the way the children were raised; the racing stables; the philanthropic oeuvres; the art collections; the flower arrangements.

In Normandy, returning with the Free French, more than once he had intervened to save women about to have their heads shaved by angry crowds, taking them under his wing and putting them in the care of local *gendarmes*. Back in Paris, a teary-eyed and frightened butler had broken the news on the landing: Baron Philippe's previous wife and mother of his only child had been deported to Germany. Early in the war, he had pleaded with her to leave but she had insisted that she was not Jewish. In the same breath, the butler had told him that his daughter, Phillipine, had been saved, although the two officers had nearly taken her as well. One of the Germans had casually remarked that he had a daughter just that age.

Baron Philippe has no peers in the collective fantasies of France. And now he's back. You can say whatever you want:

his staff were loyal during the war. At Chapon Fin, the best restaurant in Bordeaux, the one with the interior tree, the staff trade stories on their best-loved customer. Is Baron Philippe settling here or staying in Paris? Is he still an absentee landlord?

— ✦ —

Entering the mangled ruin of Greater Frankfurt, Margaret Bourke-White's Jeep must drive carefully to avoid the twisted figures of the new fallen dead. It is the living who catch her eyes. She notices women climbing out of cellars and wandering around the skeletons of houses – they are irresistibly drawn to flowers, as they fill their arms with lilacs. A moth-eaten old man stops the Jeep to explain that the horse he is leading is a military horse. Where should he take it, he asks?

— ✦ —

On 27 March, the penultimate V-2 rocket of the war destroys several buildings in Whitechapel in the East End of London, killing 134 people. Later that same day, another V-2 rocket hits Orpington in south-east London, killing a 34-year-old. The ballistic missile is 50ft long and 6ft in circumference. It rises in the air for 50–75 miles, reaching a speed of 3,600mph. Since it travels faster than the speed of sound, it gives no advance notice to the humans on the ground. In urban centers, it causes a lot of shattering fragments and flying glass, blinding many victims even before they know they have been struck.

These two V-2 ballistic missiles are Hitler's very last offensive expedients, the last two rockets fired from the European continent. The MI5 Double-Cross System keeps relaying disinformation, causing the Germans to aim at less-populated areas. No one knows that this is the last time a ballistic missile has been fired. Up until now, most V-2 rockets have hit the port of Antwerp.

V stands for *Vergeltung*, or 'retribution'. The German Volk still believes that at least one of its *Wunderwaffen* will save Germany from defeat. The Führer has developed three terrifying V weapons: the cheaply produced jet-propelled, pilotless V-1, with a range of 200–250 miles; the V-2 rocket, carrying a 1-ton warhead; and the V-3 long-range gun. All three revenge weapons predictably play an oversized role in the German imagination and in Hitler's demented psyche. He is convinced that if enough damage is inflicted in time on London, Churchill must negotiate a separate truce, allowing him to transfer divisions to the Eastern Front.

— ✦ —

Towards the end of March, 'the ice breaks' and Betty Jean Jennings receives a telegram to report quickly. She has waited the whole winter and now, in true government fashion, everything must be done quickly. Upon hearing the news, Jennings looks out the window and remembers every detail, then sits on the porch, savoring the moment.

Barely 20, she has been awarded the only degree in mathematics in her class at Northwest Missouri State Teachers' College. One of her advisors encouraged her to become a teacher. If she worked for IBM, she would simply be a cog in the wheel. Here, in Missouri, she would be a respected member of the community. Jennings wants to see something of the world. Another professor encouraged her to go to the University of Pennsylvania because they have a differential analyzer there.

Borrowing money, she arrives in Philadelphia on 30 March, stepping off the train at North Philadelphia station, unaware of the majesty of the immense Thirtieth Street station. She takes a cab to the YWCA downtown and then heads to the computing group in a beautiful old brick fraternity house. When she arrives, she meets four other women with math majors.

It's a Friday afternoon, and she must get a physical before she starts work. The doctor examines her, but says he has no time to finish and that she must come back on Monday. On Sunday afternoon, the doctor calls her at the YWCA, saying he wants to finish the physical and asking if she could come to his home. She declines and keeps her appointment for Monday. On the follow-up, the doctor is 'handsy'. Betty Jean Jennings informs her manager that they are using a lecher as a doctor.

Hired as a 'computer' with a job rating of SP-6 (sub-professional 6) and a $2,000 salary, Jennings is given an electric Monroe hand calculator and shown how to calculate each point on the arc a shell makes as it is fired from a gun. The first computing class is taught by a woman from Brooklyn, with a cigarette constantly dangling from the side of her mouth. Jennings asks a lot of questions.

April

On April Fools' Day, Stalin reassures Eisenhower by telling him that Berlin has lost its strategic importance. In Manhattan, composer John Cage and choreographer Merce Cunningham join forces and the reviewers are ecstatic.

Not far from Okinawa, a kamikaze fighter pilot gets ready for one last flight, singing his favorite school songs. President Roosevelt is felled by a stroke in the company of his former mistress. A BBC reporter in Bergen-Belsen threatens to resign.

Spending her last day in the White House and completing her chores, Eleanor Roosevelt feels free and independent. The question of FDR's legacy is preying on her mind.

In Paris, Marguerite Duras sets up a tracing service for returnees at the Gare d'Orsay. From San Francisco, a young John F. Kennedy files newspaper articles for the Hearst Corporation on the first United Nations conference, but his heart is not really in it. Beautiful women don't give a damn about journalists.

In his Berlin bunker, Adolf Hitler makes good on his promise to marry Eva Braun.

On the morning of 1 April, Stalin is in a good mood. He asks his two most hard-hitting generals, Koniev and Zhukov, 'Well, who's going to take Berlin: we or the Allies?'

Koniev is the quickest, 'It's we who'll take Berlin!'

Zhukov hasn't had time to respond.

'So that's the sort of man you are?' Stalin smiles at Koniev. That same day, the Soviet leader reassures Eisenhower by telling him that Berlin has lost its former strategic importance.

— ✦ —

On 5 April, John Cage and Merce Cunningham give their first concert together. Cunningham designed the costumes, Cage designed the printed program, and they shared expenses to advertise the concert and to rent the small Studio Theatre on West Sixteenth Street. The reviews in New York are ecstatic. *Dance Observer* calls it 'a brilliant and deserved success'. In the *Tribune*, an impressed critic admits that he has never seen 'a first recital that combined such impeccable taste … such technical finish, such originality of dance material'.

How did they pull it off? Spectators were treated to six short piano dances by Cunningham. The composer and choreographer agreed beforehand to start and end each agreed-upon unit together and in between they would work separately. Such a combination of rhythmic structure and open-ended lightness. Such marvelous freedom.

— ✦ —

On 12 April, singing hymns at dawn, kamikaze pilot Hayashi Ichizō heads to Okinawa on his last mission. Aged 23, a graduate of the Imperial University of Kyoto, Ichizō has the rank of navy ensign. Shortly before his last flight, he goes for a walk in a field of Chinese milk vetch (*rengesō*) and lies down, thinking about home and his short life. Cherry blossoms of the Yoshino variety have fallen and double-petaled cherry blossoms are blooming right before his eyes. People have been so good to me, Ichizō thinks. He notices a yellow rose blooming on a fence that is wet from rain. He washes his face in a brook.

— ✦ —

'I have a terrible pain in the back of my head,' Roosevelt says. The president elicits lots of lively interest. He has planned to relax in the sunshine of Warm Springs, Georgia, and that Thursday afternoon, 12 April, he is scheduled to see a dress rehearsal of a minstrel show with an all-polio-patient cast. In late April, he plans to go to San Francisco to give the opening address at the United Nations organization. He also looks forward to a celebratory visit to England. FDR is holding his newspaper when he begins to rub his temple, before awkwardly watching his left arm fall.

Further north in Washington, Eleanor Roosevelt is sitting at the exclusive Sulgrave Club for a fundraiser when one of the ladies tiptoes up to her and whispers in her ear to take an urgent phone call. She decides to wait until the pianist is finished. The call is from FDR's press secretary, Steve Early, asking her to go home as soon as possible. In her heart, she knows, and she sits with clenched hands all the way to the White House, not daring to formulate these terrible thoughts until they are spoken.

The president is dead. For twelve years he had led America out of the Great Depression and implemented the New Deal in response to the worst economic crisis in American history. Most Americans imagined that the president would be alive on Victory Day. From the White House, Eleanor calls President Truman, asking him whether it would be appropriate to take a government plane down south. The request is instantly granted.

She arrives in Warm Springs just before midnight. Upon arriving at the Little White House, Eleanor is stunned to find out that Lucy Mercer Rutherford, FDR's former mistress, had been present at the time of her husband's brain hemorrhage.

— ✦ —

A distant rumble of mechanical warfare can be heard in the distance. On Sunday, 15 April, everyone is present for roll call on the square of Bergen-Belsen. It's nine o'clock, the sacred hour. Despite a cold breeze, the weather is co-operating somehow, with sunshine warming bodies. The immaculate masters of Dora, the *kapos* and barrack chiefs and other lower nobility are ready to proceed. The emaci-ated old hands make every effort to remain upright. They and the tottering wretches are all present. Throats tighten. From the moment they got up, they could hear beyond the barbed wire the rapid patter of machine guns, artillery fire, and odd, isolated shots. This is indeed the season of the wildest hopes.

How far away are the Allied army units now? What will happen next? Will this be a signal for the SS to murder the prisoners en masse?

Roll call is the very essence of what camp life is all about, and there is no reason it should not take place today. An imperturbable SS *Blockführer* approaches the rows of *Häftlinge* and begins counting. Scarecrow silhouettes are well lined up. At the end of every column, the number of the night's dead is added – fine, the numbers tally.

My God! From the corners of their eyes, prisoners distin-guish mechanical monsters with cannons aimed at the barbed wire. The first one crushes the gate, and immediately behind him a small car armed with a machine gun and a soldier with a flat helmet, his finger on the trigger – an Englishman. This is it. An enormous clamor rises above the camp, a sound never heard in history, gushing from every throat. *Free! Alive!*

Amid cries of joy and shouts of rage, the SS draw their guns. They start firing as they make a quick exit. *Kapos* and barrack chiefs start running across the square, but armed with clubs, they are no match for angry prisoners.

The Russians instantly get into the action. Cries of hatred and murder. Cries of vengeance coming from hollow, infected chests.

An uncomprehending armlet-wearer tries to restore order, '*Ruhe!*' The mandate is imperative; the urge irrepressible. He is hellbent on providing the exact count of prisoners to the SS. He furiously blows his whistle. He wants the clock to go back in time. Surrounded, he cries for help. He disappears under an angry crowd that pummels him. When it stands back, one of his eyes is out of its socket. A man picks up heavy lumber to crush his head. The limbs are shuddering. The legs twitch sporadically. A Russian undoes his fly and urinates on the body.

Besides this collective pent-up rage that needs to find an outlet, an equally vast undercurrent grips the newly liberated prisoners. Men are crying with joy – intensely brilliant cries of joys. Their first urge is not vengeance but finding old friends, laughter rising on their ruined faces.

The liberators have seen their fair share of dehumanization and death. They have seen torn limbs in trees and disemboweled friends, but never anything like this. The tank crews open their trapdoors to take a closer look, but this is beyond the insufferable. They feel sick. But the sun is still rising. It will be a fine day.

— ◆ —

Richard Dimbleby breaks down five times while recording his report from Belsen. For several days, his BBC bosses refuse to believe or broadcast it until he threatens to resign.

Bergen-Belsen victims. (US Army Signal Corps, Harry S. Truman Library & Museum, NAID: 348448293 / 72-3277)

— ✦ —

On 20 April, Eleanor Roosevelt completes her chores, spending her last day at the White House. The Roosevelts had lived here for twelve years. It's the passing of an era – or is it? The upstairs rooms look desolate. She has packed twenty trunks of Roosevelt possessions, carefully setting aside her private correspondence to her dearest friends.

Three days earlier, she hosted a farewell tea party for the women of her press corps, answering questions, saying that nothing would induce her to run for public office or accept an appointment at the present time. Relieved from political responsibilities, she feels free and alone. Upon her arrival at her Washington Square flat, she dismisses reporters, saying, 'The story is over.'

Nevertheless, in the corners of her busy mind, Eleanor Roosevelt cannot refrain from wondering what her husband's most profound legacy was. Her daily column 'My Day' awaits. It is syndicated in approximately ninety newspapers and runs six times a week.

His very last words, written on 11 April but not delivered the next day, had thrilled her. This type of oratory is so reminiscent of his first inaugural speech. In his last message, he had stated that the mere conquest of our enemies was not enough. Ignorance and greed had made this horror possible. 'Today we are faced with the pre-eminent fact that, if civilization is to survive, we must cultivate the science of human relationships – the ability of all people, of all kinds, to live together and work together in the same world, at peace.' And now, 'The work, my friends, is peace'. Eleanor now realizes that calling this conference while the war was still raging was an excellent idea. If the forty-four nations invited to San Francisco could set up a durable Charter, this would give hope. And so now, part of her thinks that this abiding wish, this quest for peace in a united world, is the only way to go forward.

In her 'My Day' column, Eleanor builds an unassailable syllogism. At a time when grief pervades the world and personal sorrow seems to be lost in the general sadness of humanity, there is only one way 'to repay the dead who have given their utmost for the cause of liberty and justice'. FDR's goal had been to build an international organization to prevent future wars. This is now her own quest: to avoid repeating the horrors of the past.

Eleanor is well aware that a world without war is a chimera if entire nations or disadvantaged minorities lack access to basic security – food, work, education, health. But the practical idealist in her believes that with enough goodwill, old ideas of empire and master-race superiority and certain kinds of mad leadership might yield to a new political system. We must boldly create a new system of fairness and dignity. There has to be a way to live peacefully and co-operatively, internationally and within our own borders.

— ◆ —

Friday, 20 April. Marguerite Duras sets up a tracing service for returnees at the Gare d'Orsay. Wives of prisoners congeal in a solid mass behind white barriers. They keep asking, 'Do you have any news of so-and-so?' They wait for the trucks turning off the Solferino Bridge.

There are, in fact, two crowds of women. Those who shout out names of prisoners when they disembark, and those who come as spectators to see how the men back from Germany are greeted. 'Kassel?', 'VII A?', 'III A Kommando?' – one hears the names of German towns and Stalag numbers as the French citizens drop out of the trucks.

— ◆ —

Jack Kennedy, the ambassador's son, is as thin as a rake. His health is awful. Jack is reporting from the West Coast on the birth of the United Nations for Hearst Newspapers. Having fought the war in the Pacific, he is glad to hear the clang of trolleys on the streets of San Francisco. He sees GIs crowding the place, and it's a good feeling. When he interviews them on street corners, most of them don't seem to have a clear-cut conception of what this international conference is trying to achieve. 'I don't know much about what's going on but – if they just fix it so we don't have to fight any more – they can count on me.'

Jack is wearing a brace and doesn't look robust. Because of his bad back, he spends a lot of time in his room at the Palace Hotel. He makes sure to take long showers to soothe his backbone. In bed, he enjoys women on top of him. He has a wry sense of humor, and people like to be around him, even when he lacks energy.

Jack worries about the superior status of figures like 'Chip' Bohlen and Averell Harriman – those who were present at

Yalta. Adlai Stevenson proves to be an entertaining public speaker, and women also gravitate to him. These men can't be described as romantic rivals, but they have more power. New England women are focused on pedigree. Women in Hollywood care for artistic genius. In San Francisco, 'roving ambassadors' are popular. Here in San Francisco, JFK is one of 2,500 press, radio, and newsreel representatives from many societies and organizations. He is a mere journalist-observer.

Every press conference convinces him that this large international gathering is doomed to be merely a skeleton with limited powers. Molotov is as uninformative and uncooperative as a Russian can be. He knows they are going to pick a fight on every little issue in the hope they can write their own terms on the big ones. After gaining acceptance of the Ukrainian and White Russian delegations, they request that a delegation from the Lublin Polish Communist Government (as it is now constituted) be seated among the other delegations. Edward Stettinius Jr jumps to his feet and makes sure he greenlights a Human Rights Commission.

Jack is dressed for a black-tie evening. Apart from his pumps and evening coat, he is propped up on three pillows, a highball in one hand and the telephone receiver in the other, talking to the operator. 'Not in?'

Pause.

'Well, put someone on to take a message.'

Another pause.

'Can you see that the boss gets this message as soon as you can reach him? Thank you. Here's the message: "Kennedy will not be filing tonight."'

— ◆ —

Hitler is getting ready for his midnight wedding. He has barely seen any daylight in two months. He used to work in the Reich

Chancellery until the US Air Force turned Berlin into a five-day fireball in early February 1945. After that, the Führer retreated to his two underground bunkers. One is an air-raid shelter built directly beneath the cellars of the Reich Chancellery; the other, the Führer bunker proper, is located 10 yards below the Chancellery Garden with a 3-yard-thick concrete roof.

Now the Russians have broken through the inner cordon north of Berlin. The heavy shelling and mortar fire place the bunker under siege and leave it completely isolated.

On his fifty-sixth birthday, 20 April 1945, Hitler sees daylight for the last time, as he greets members of the Hitler Youth and encourages them in a final attempt to stop the Red Army. A picture shows him touching the cheek of a Hitler Youth and the forearm of another. Both continue to look straight ahead as instructed. The image will become famous.

At midnight, local time, a nervous civil magistrate, former Gau inspector Walter Wagner, stands in front of Eva Braun and Adolf Hitler. It's a wartime wedding and brief on formalities. Only declarations are needed. She is dressed in a long, black, silk taffeta dress and wearing exclusive black Ferragamo shoes. Her lovely face reminds the wedding guests of simpler times at Berchtesgaden when one could still gaze upon the untouched landscapes that made Germany so beautiful.

Her husband-to-be is wearing his traditional gray military jacket and black trousers. His skin now grayish, his face deathly pale, and his body slightly stooped, the Reichsführer of Greater Germany, the hero of countless propaganda newsreels, looks old. He is no longer the figure who stood at the top of the gigantic staircase at Nuremberg Fields surrounded by dignitaries in front of an oversized swastika. He no longer embodies a 1,000-year Reich. Yet when he locks on you with his eyes, he can still exude that mesmerizing power.

Smarting from the ingratitude of the German people, Adolf Hitler has now decided to transfer his allegiance to

A portrait of Eva Braun.
(NARA NAID: 266695137
/ 306-NT-295J-1)

From Eva Braun's photo album, which was taken by Americans and brought
back to the US. The album is now at the National Archives and Records
Administration (NARA). (NARA NAID: 540149 / 242-EB)

one woman. He had warned his *Volk* a year earlier that if the German people could not wrest victory from the enemy, then they would be destroyed. They deserve to perish, for the best of Germany's manhood will have fallen in battle. Germany's end will be horrible, and the German people will have deserved it.

The officiating magistrate asks the couple to confirm that they are of pure Aryan descent and free of any hereditary disease. Hitler's lineage is murky, to say the least, and his real name is difficult to pronounce. When it comes to hereditary diseases, Hitler suffers from an undescended testicle and penile hypospadias, his urethra opening on the underside of his penis. In the past, he injected himself with bovine testosterone before sex, and for a long time, the future bride had to take special medication to spare *Mein Führer* the sight of menstruations.

The bride begins to sign 'Eva Braun' but strikes out the initial 'B' and signs instead 'Eva Hitler, née Braun'. Hitler's signature is almost illegible.

During the small wedding party, Hitler allows himself a glass of sweetened Hungarian wine. He is a teetotaler, but why not? Guests share champagne, liverwurst, and biscuits. While they engage in small talk, Hitler re-enters his secretary's office to look at the final draft of his political and his personal testament.

In his political testament, Hitler sacks key officials, accusing them of treacherous behavior and of suing for peace with the Allies without his consent. In his personal testament, Hitler donates his paintings – many stolen from the cities his forces have conquered – to the museum in Linz, his birthplace. Architect Speer had drawn up blueprints for a museum the size of the Reichstag, where the Führer's life would be mythologized for millions of adoring Germans.

To those still close to him, Hitler remains a perpetual *Wunder.* What a career! He had come once to Vienna as a young provincial because, as he said, he 'wanted to be something'. There he had learned a new kind of politics. He remained true to his obsessive vilification of international Jewry until the end. He had outwitted Catholics and Protestants, tamed Ruhr industrialists, seduced Prussian landowners, struck backroom deals with German conservatives, overruled his generals, and triumphed with Blitzkrieg victories in the West. He had continued his high-risk strategies by invading the endless Eurasian landmass. *Dummkopf.* Then, they admit ruefully, he lost it all when he lunged for the Volga and the Baku oil fields instead of focusing on Moscow, and then foolishly declared war against American industrialism. *Jackass.*

The Führer signs his political and personal testaments, and couriers distribute copies to the new military commanders in the field and to Party Headquarters in Munich. At five in the morning, the newlyweds retire to their bedroom.

— ✦ —

At 6.30 a.m. on 29 April, in Hitler's upper bunker, a young officer, Bernd Freytag von Loringhoven, is whispering with his roommate, Gerhard Boldt. They are trading news about the previous day's events. The two share a small room, which is partitioned off by a curtain from General Krebs, who is still asleep. Their job is to prepare twice-daily reports for their commanding officer. Everything has to be sugarcoated with talk of stabilizing the front. The young officers desperately want to be sent on a combat mission – out of 'the morgue'. With Hitler alive, there can be no negotiations. The Russian guns are now within 500 yards.

Boldt and von Loringhoven trade gallows' humor. Apparently, one of the secretaries went to the Chancellery upstairs and came down screaming about people engaged in lascivious behavior, unlimited amounts of alcohol, and taking turns in the dentist's chair. 'You may safely call me Frau Hitler.' It's pure nervous energy. They are at their wit's end. They adopt Austrian speech mannerisms, '*Gnädiges Fraulein*'. From behind the curtain, they hear the voice of their commanding officer, 'Have you taken leave of your senses, gentlemen, laughing so disrespectfully at the sovereign leader of your country?'

By midday, von Loringhoven and his friend are desperate to leave the bunker. Freytag means to save his life. During the morning conference, just after eleven in the morning, von Loringhoven and Boldt suggest to General Krebs that now that the telecommunications are down, they should make direct contact with General Wenck. They will urge him to break through the city ahead of the Twelfth Army to stabilize the front and spearhead the attack. Krebs is not convinced, but he likes the sound of 'stabilizing the front'. At least von Loringhoven is not making ridiculous promises of an impregnable Berlin and the inevitable victory.

The proposal makes some sense now that communications are down. Burgdorf appears, asking if he is ready for a drink. He appreciates this latest initiative and suggests his adjutant Rudolph Weiss tag along. Then Bormann comes in for a glass of schnapps and he too endorses it. So far so good.

In fact, no one in the bunker knows that General Walther Wenck has no desire to defend the capital. All he wants to do is keep a corridor open for soldiers and civilians, especially girls. Parents cannot protect their daughters. There is no other talk in the city.

At 12.30 p.m., Krebs tries to sell the idea of a contact mission to Wenck to Hitler himself. The Führer wants to see the officers.

At the back of the room, Nicolaus von Below carefully watches these 'escape artists' at work with their Houdini trick. He is familiar with the geography of Berlin.

Von Below also wants out. He longs for his pregnant wife and children stationed on the Baltic coast. He knows that if Freytag von Loringhoven asks clumsily, permission will be refused – high-stakes poker. Von Loringhoven calmly points to several possible route options on a large map laid out on the table. The aim is to reach Pichelsdorf Bridge outside Berlin and from there travel down the River Havel in a rowing boat.

Silence.

Hitler likes this boat idea and now orders Bormann to supply the officers with a motorboat. The Führer always has the last word, and it is no use arguing with him. Nicolaus von Below notes that, yet again, Hitler is completely out of his depth.

Von Loringhoven says, '*Mein Führer*, we will get hold of a motorboat ourselves and deaden the noise. I'm convinced we will get through.'

Hitler slowly gets to his feet. 'Give my regards to Wenck. Tell him to hurry or it will be too late.'

Von Loringhoven responds, '*Jawohl, mein Führer.*'

May

In Berlin, war correspondent Vassily Grossman should be happy. The Red Flag flutters over the Reichstag in Berlin but thousands of women are raped every day. Further south, Reich Minister of Aviation Hermann Göring sips champagne from a balcony and waves amicably at American journalists.

In Norway, red, blue, and white flags splash out in the streets. Oslo looks like an impressionist painting. Yes, people are weeping in joy. Anne Sommerhausen, a Belgian resistance worker, observes her sleepy husband.

Staff sergeant at the Counterintelligence Corps (CIC), J.D. Salinger, struggles with signs of a nervous breakdown. On 13 May, he writes a cracked letter home: a tricky, dreary farce, that's what it is.

Two lowly American officers track down Albert Speer in a castle. A surgeon hears of an outbreak of typhus at the Dachau Camp and wants to get a closer look.

It is 2 May. The Red Flag flies over the Reichstag. A liberated French POW comes up to Vassily Grossman. 'Monsieur,' he says, 'I like your army and that is why it is painful for me to see how it is treating girls and women. It is going to do great harm to your propaganda.'

Grossman winces and for a moment the two Communists stare at one another. The liberated French POW does not speak with false cordiality. Comrade to comrade, with a disdainful tone. It is an earth-shattering indictment of the Red Army.

Right now, Vassily Grossman is on the streets of Berlin on the day of the German surrender. Much of the city is in flames. He has just seen two lovers on a bench in the Tiergarten, acting like they were the last people on earth. The zookeeper's gorillas are dead. 'Humans,' he tells Grossman, 'are more ferocious than animals.' As Grossman enters Hitler's lair, he sees Russian soldiers making bonfires in the hall. He picks up rubber stamps that say 'The Fuhrer has confirmed' and 'The Fuhrer has agreed'.

Reporting for *Krasnaya Zvezda*, Grossman has had a productive war. In the first days of the war, he learned the true art of front-line reporting, where every soldier is another's equal, and maybe better than a general. He writes, not to be admired or believed, but with the single-minded, Kremlin-inspired purpose of pouring many more millions into the cauldron of battle to win the Great Patriotic War.

Grossman – a typical Moscow intelligentsia name – is a sad figure. He battles his own dark mindset, blaming himself for not getting his mother out of Berdichev in time. Early on, he had a premonition. He is one of the first journalists in world history writing on unfathomable massacres in Ukraine. He tells his readers that the quiet in the empty villages is much more frightening than the tears and curses.

In Berlin, the screams are heard from open windows. The horror in the eyes of German women and children, and the stories of gang rapes. The black bruises on their necks and

An office in the ruins of Berlin at the end of the Second World War. (Harry S. Truman Library & Museum NAID 350877684)

faces and swollen eyes are impossible to miss. They do not speak Russian and that makes it easier. *You just do your stuff and go away.* When the women bleed or lose consciousness, they are shoved to one side.

Grossman will be felled by a massive nervous breakdown when he returns to Moscow. Recovering slowly, the same war correspondent thinks hard on the randomness of fate. Ever so slowly, his willpower returns. A part of him wants to tackle large ethical questions on the nature of war, but how? Ever so slowly *Life and Fate*, a modern update of Tolstoy's *War and Peace*, coalesces in his mind.

— ◆ —

On 6 May, surrounded by SS officers at Berchtesgaden, Hermann Göring hears the news of Hitler's death on the radio. Distraught, Göring says to his wife, Eddy, 'Now I can no

Cheering crowds on a lorry in Oslo, 8 May 1945. (Photographer: Ingvald Møllerstad, Aftenposten, Creative Commons)

'We are the Victors!', 8 May 1945. Location unknown. (Norway State Archive, Bergen: Jacobsen, Leon and Birgit Collection)

longer vindicate myself. I can never look him in the face and tell him that he wronged me, that I remained loyal to him.' The SS are supposed to shoot him, but this radio announcement saps their will.

On a traffic-jammed road, Göring surrenders to the first American he meets: First Lieutenant Jerome Shapiro, a Jewish officer from New York. Göring and his family are transferred to Schloss Fischhorn, where they settle in private rooms on the second floor of the castle. Göring keeps reassuring his wife that all will be well: he is slated to meet Eisenhower, in his words, 'Marshal to Marshal'.

At US Seventh Army Headquarters in Augsburg, the mood is reminiscent of the First World War, with flying aces and war heroes praising one another and pointing with mock humor at their medals: 'Look, *Pour Le Mérite*.' Göring appears on the balcony surrounded by high-ranking American officers. Below, the photographers' shutters click.

When General Eisenhower hears of Göring's reception, he immediately orders that he be treated as an ordinary prisoner of war. The search for hidden arms, weapons, and poisons begins, and Göring is transferred to the Interrogation Center. An impromptu press conference takes place outside. The former head of the German Air Force is to be tried as a war criminal.

During the war he was mobbed by youth as he distributed toy planes and tanks to poor children. His Stukas had subdued Poland, the Netherlands, Belgium, and France in co-ordinated Blitzkrieg attacks. Days before, he evacuated his collection of stolen art to Berchtesgaden in six railroad cars. One hour, he is treated with respect; the next, he is regarded as a buffoon.

— ✦ —

Peace Day – 8 May – starts in Oslo with impulsive rejoicing. Norwegian flags are flying everywhere. Tens of thousands pour into the streets, and again and again sing the national anthem *'Ja, vi elsker'*. Many weep uncontrollably. The New Police blossom in their blue uniforms. Tram conductors do not collect fares. Children are everywhere to be seen. Victory is ours! We have won!

— ◆ —

Donald A. Lowrie and his wife Helen specialize in humanitarian work – more specifically, in saving 'hunted children'. Before they decide to drive out of Geneva to make their way back to Paris, they listen to the radio announcing that the German surrender is expected. Despite the broadcast warning not to be impatient, the lovely weather highlights the new green crops and noticeable towns and villages. One can see people putting up flags on their houses and happy-faced little groups at street corners. Stopping for the night at a tiny hotel in Auxerre, they finally hear the good news.

Paris is a scene of brilliant sunshine and crowded streets. Lowrie and his wife have only enough time to quickly deposit their baggage in the apartment at United States House. They hurry across town to the thanksgiving ceremony at the Chaillot Palace, right across from the sparkling *Tour Eiffel*. Inside, across the stage, the only decoration is the line of Allied flags against a dark-velvet curtain. There is an army band and the splendid soldiers' choir sings twice. Next, they listen to a dozen brief addresses. The ceremony is 'infinitely deep and moving' and a 'peculiarly fitting recognition of the historic moment'.

Outside, the sirens sound the 'all clear'. The wild rejoicing, the shouting, the hugging and the dancing contrasts with the simple dignity of the solemn ceremony indoors. Raising their heads, they can see the sunlit sky and hundreds of parading aircraft. Later that night, there will be plenty of fireworks. During this show, 'Your Service of Thanksgiving', Lowrie tries not to think of the past but is bracing himself for the task of reconstruction for years ahead.

Lowrie's humanitarian work had started during his service to prisoners in Siberia in 1916. During the dark years of German occupation, armed with a regulation passport and a travel permit, Lowrie had spent many days in stuffy Vichy anterooms. He tried to obtain necessary documents for stateless *apatrides* and persecuted *indésirables* in Vichy France.

His first efforts had led him to Gur — a sea of mud in the Pyrénées, where survivors of the Spanish Civil War were dying at an alarming rate. Then he had tried to find supplies for devoted Cimade midwives in prisoner camps. Most of his time as the head of the Nîmes Committee had been spent trying to shake the apathy of the Swiss Red Cross behemoth and obtaining official permits and passes, affidavits, vaccination certificates, travel documents, and identification bracelets for children. *Yes, he was an American representing a well-known organization. Yes, the North American YMCA.* He had faced many a stony-faced and inquisitorial civil servant.

Thanks to Cardinal Gerlier, he had managed to place children in Catholic welfare agencies. Through an intermediary, he had several times tried to meet with Maréchal Pétain as trains packed with Jews were being transferred to unknown destinations to the east, which would later be known as concentration camps. And he had witnessed scenes of infinite suffering when parents had to release their children to some welfare agency on the eve of a planned deportation. In the end, with the help of *Œuvre de secours aux enfants* (OSE), he had saved 5,000 children, but a slightly greater number of children had been deported.

At the Chaillot Palace, Lowrie could only think of the future, and what needed to be done in the coming years. The past and the present were far too painful.

— ✦ —

On Saturday morning, 12 May, Anne Somerhausen, a Belgian resistance worker, is in bed. She observes her sleeping husband. She notices the deep wrinkles on his face. She is trying to read the stories the lines tell. His face is tanned by the sun. He does not sense that she is studying him. He sleeps profoundly. At times, there is a twitching around his mouth.

He had said goodbye five years ago to the day, almost to the hour. No word came through in the last eight months of the war, and she had wondered whether she was a widow. Would she fight on alone forever?

When he came home, he used his own latchkey to open the door and walked straight to the garden. This key was his talisman, he said. In the garden, he recognized one of his two sons. 'Is this Luke?' he asked.

'Are you my dad?' the boy responded.

His hands are harder and broader. He is asleep. *He is here. My work is done. All, all is well.*

— ✦ —

On 13 May, J.D. Salinger writes an unsettling letter home. His mind is unhinged. Alternating between raw sarcasm and full-strength despondency, he admits that his most casual thoughts are testy and subversive. 'It's a mess Elizabeth. Wonder if you have any idea.' He adds that he was delighted that he missed the VE Day celebrations in the United States, especially the ticker-tape parade in New York. Not for him, the 'sight of thousands [of] patriotic garment workers throwing raw woolens out of the windows'. On the day Germany surrendered, he wrote, 'I celebrated the day wondering what close relatives would think if I fired a .45 slug neatly, but effectively through the palm of my left hand.' In the next paragraph, his mood plummets still further: 'I have three battle participation stars and am due a fourth, and I intend to have them all grafted onto my nostrils, two on each side. What a tricky, dreary farce, and how many are dead.'

— ◆ —

Two officers from an advance party of the American Strategic Bombing Survey have now tracked down Hitler's Minister of Armaments and Production. They find him on 15 May 1945 at 1.30 p.m. at Schloss Glücksburg, by the Danish border. It is a splendid edifice, surrounded by a moat and a lake. The American lieutenant enters the castle and asks, 'Do you know where Speer is?'

The man responds, 'This is me. How can I help you?'

The good Nazi, Albert Speer is tall and slender, with dark, slightly sparse hair and a mobile, sometimes amused face. He has taken up living quarters in this sixteenth-century castle complete with butlers, soldiers, and secretaries. Speer proves extremely co-operative. For more than three hours, First Lieutenant Wolfgang G. Sklarz and Technical Sergeant Harold E. Fassberg carry out the first 'debriefing'.

'*Berthold Konrad Hermann Albert Speer, born at 11.15 a.m. on 19 March 1905 in Mannheim.*'

'Is this how you spell it?' he asks. Translation issues need to be ironed out.

Speer started out as an architect, working on the decor of the Nazi Party rally in the Nuremberg Stadium. Speer makes hand gestures. How do you translate that? 'Dome of light'? He had arrayed anti-aerial searchlights to pierce the night sky. He was with the Führer as a tourist to Paris in 1940, a brief one-day visit. Speer quickly notices that the Americans know very little about the inner workings of the Third Reich: 'The Führer wanted a gigantic new Reichstag, and he picked me as his architect.'

Yes, they spent time together at Berchtesgaden and on trains.

'The Führer liked to look at my blueprints.'

He got up late and then liked to work on his speeches. He was a teetotaler. No coffee, no tea. He didn't smoke. He couldn't ride a horse. He couldn't drive a car.

After the accidental death in a plane crash of Fritz Todt, Hitler's construction chief, the Führer had appointed Speer as minister. He had reorganized the economy, led the technological war, and solved the transportation crisis. No, he didn't know anything about forced labor in concentration camps.

Speer's eyes glaze over, recalling that photograph of him at Mauthausen, where he visited on 30 March 1943. He had written a letter to Himmler afterwards to complain about the 'luxurious' construction standards he had seen there.

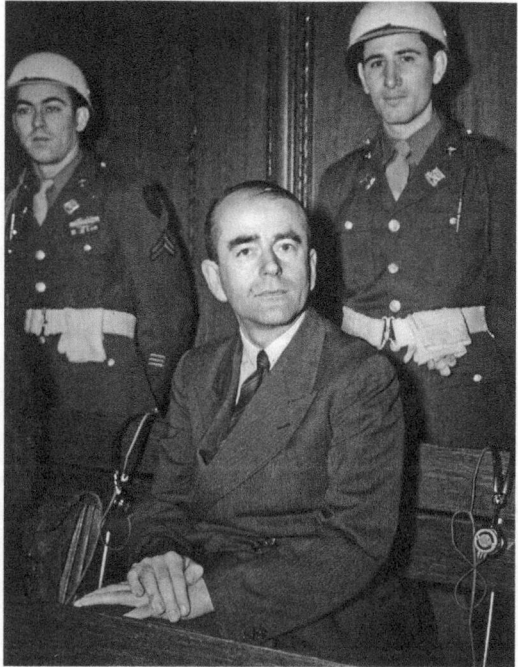

Albert Speer, Minister of Production, at the Nuremberg War Crime Trials. (NAID: 348449309 Local ID: 72-929)

Next, Speer dwells at length on the impact of the aerial raids on the Ruhr and the raids on Hamburg. Yes, he was in Hitler's bunker in April 1945 – the Führer's rigidity and exhaustion; his nonsensical rhetoric of Aryan heroism and anti-Semitism; the slaughter of the war. Speer says he opposed and frustrated the Führer's scorched-earth policies and almost plotted to gas him and his henchmen. Can you *almost* plot, the Americans wonder.

The interview is over. The two subaltern American interrogators are pleased because Speer has a complete picture of the German war effort. His memory is astounding. Additionally, he shows great pride in the results achieved by German production while under his control. Speer has also offered to share his personal papers, stored in a safe in Hamburg.

Doesn't this man realize the game is up? Maybe this is why he's so courteous? He makes no effort to distance himself from his Führer. The interrogators thank him.

— ◆ —

Combat surgeon Brendan Phibbs obtains permission from the division surgeon and his commanding officer to travel to the Dachau concentration camp. He drives his ambulance down the autobahn past Augsburg to the outskirts of Munich. He looks forward to working on typhus, a rare and almost legendary disease, an acute necrotizing process in the cells of the capillaries throughout the body. He reckons only a handful of physicians in the United States have ever seen typhus. He wants to learn and see with his own eyes that swift inflammation and degeneration with catastrophic results.

At the hospital, he is dusted with DDT. The typhus ward seems bigger than a gymnasium, with long rows of cots inches apart. Rasping voices keep clamoring for attention. As he begins daily rounds and patient care, he is frequently accompanied by two former inmates.

One is an elderly Dutch physician who prides himself on being a Communist. He is still in his blue-striped pajamas, which flutter loosely around his feeble frame. Having spent the war in Dachau, he is a collection of bones and is barely mobile. He will not accept more food than the patients. To accept extra food is a betrayal of his friends.

The other is a recent graduate from the University of Belgrade. He is in good health and recovering fast. During his brief army career in the mountains of Yugoslavia, he lived with typhus in the lousy encampments of partisans. He is delighted to be called 'Tito Minor' and goes out of his way to share his knowledge of the classic symptoms.

Walking down the wards, it's plain to see that the patients are desperately hungry. They try to grab the doctors' sleeves. They triangulate in several languages to be understood. Tito Minor, meanwhile, looks attentively at the smallest manifestations of the disease. He teaches the American surgeon to look for the classic symptoms, namely rapid heartbeat and falling blood pressure, proof that the blood system is invaded. The disease begins with a fever, then a deep-pink eruption that blanches under light pressure, followed by dark hemorrhagic speckles all over the body. When patients start to babble wildly and gesticulate, they will be dead within twenty-four hours. Their ends come with convulsions and agonal screaming. 'Soon dead', Tito Minor is invariably right.

As they move between patients, persistent moans of 'hunger, hunger' dog the doctors' steps. 'Herr Major, we are starving. I don't believe this.' The only real treatment on offer is food but some criminal Third Army satrap, some flaming ass in the quartermaster corps, has forbidden the feeding of GI rations to foreign civilians. A meal, then, consists of a cup of milk and two crackers from a K ration. The patients comment with bitter irony to one another, '*Guten Appetit!*'

June

Stalin thinks Hitler is still alive. British, American, French, Canadian, and Belgian intelligence services co-operate to track down the Führer's close aides to describe Hitler's last days prior to his suicide.

Some painters continue to paint as though there never was a war. Pierre Bonnard locks himself into his bathroom to paint the contours of a bathtub and the reflections of water yet again on the tiles. Sometimes, he places a small dog next to the relaxed, elongated naked body in the water.

Arrested in Berlin, Major Heinz Knappe is now a prisoner of war. Because of his access to Nazi bigwigs, he is about to board an airplane to Moscow for forwarding to a special camp where interrogators will have a go at him. His wartime journey to Moscow in 1941 took several months. This one should take four hours.

The Office of Wartime Information (OWI) in Washington DC starts to scale down propaganda and public relations campaigns. In New Zealand, the countryside is a mix of ice and wet snow, gray skies, and damp weather. The Land Girls in New Zealand receive a 10 shillings per week pay rise.

On this day, 6 June, Stalin tells Truman's envoy that he is sure Hitler is still alive. He claims that the Allies are conspiring to hide Hitler in the British Zone. He acknowledges that the bodies of Joseph Goebbels and his wife have been found but denies finding the remains of Hitler and Eva Braun. Three days later, on 9 June, at a press conference in Germany, Marshal Zhukov tells journalists that no corpse which could be identified as Adolf Hitler has been found.

Hitler could have left Berlin at the last moment. In his opinion, Hitler has gone into hiding, possibly with Franco. The Soviet news agency, TASS, next announces that Hitler has been spotted in Dublin, disguising himself in women's clothing.

On 5 May, members of the Soviet military counter-espionage team known as SMERSH dig up Hitler's charred remains. On 11 May, a technician who had made Hitler's dentures confirmed that the body was indeed the Führer's. This positive evidence was relayed on 31 May to Laventi Beria in Moscow, who in turn ordered that this report be passed on to Stalin.

Germans and Fascists everywhere need to be reminded that their Führer is no more. Germany cannot recover if the shadow of Hitler hovers above the country. Hitler needs to be dead for healing and reconstruction to begin. Germans will not regain a historical perspective of a catastrophic war as long as rumors of Hitler's whereabouts throttle general enquiries.

British, American, French, Canadian, and Belgian intelligence services co-operate to track down close aides to describe his last days. They call on the Field Security Police and the administrations of prisoner-of-war camps to carry out special enquiries. The mystery of Hitler's death is a scandal. Human observers agree: the proof of his death is urgently needed. It's a work of some considerable historic significance.

— ◆ —

Pierre Bonnard's *Nude in the Bath and Small Dog*. (Carnegie Museum of Art, Wikimedia Commons)

Suspended time. Pierre Bonnard paints his last canvas devoted to the subject of *Nude in the Bath*. People taking a bath are to him what water lilies are to Monet. Bonnard doesn't watch to catch the fleeting moment, but rather the duration of the bath, the quilt of water, the harmonious cords surrounding the body of his wife, Marthe.

Bonnard started this painting in 1941. She passed away the following year, but he keeps painting her. This painting doesn't just point at the bath but includes the entire bathroom. The oval and the square angles of the bathroom itself are on the verge of disintegrating. In the front is a light bath mat on which lies his dachshund, Poucette, looking at the viewer. The left foot of the bather stretches to the oval rim of the bathtub. The immaculate white enamel has turned into a light blue, contrasted with the bright yellow, deep orange, violent purple and green tiles: pure lozenges of color! Marthe's body dissolves in the play of reflections. A visionary transformation full of anguish, a crystalline chamber of suspended time.

— ✦ —

In the suburb of Berlin near Rüdersdorf, 1,000 German prisoners of war are put behind barbed wire. One of them is Siegfried Knappe, who with General Weidling negotiated with Chuikov the terms of surrender in the ruins of Berlin, having visited the Hitler bunker several times. Knappe is now a marked man in the sense that he will be questioned intensively back in Moscow.

In the Berlin compound, there is access to water and decent toilet facilities but no soap. Major Knappe tries to suppress any thoughts about losing the war, the wrong turns and strategic mistakes. He regularly shares coffee and good cigars with Major Wolff. Every day, they spend a quiet hour smoking the Dutch Ritmeester brand. Next, he is driven in a Jeep to a 'gentlemen's prison' with some general staff officers. Observing how the guards patrol on each side of the house, Knappe decides to escape on a moonless night, then swim across the river to hide in a gardener's shed. During breakfast, he is told he is a lucky man, 'You are going to Moscow!'

At Tempelhof Airport he is put on board an American DC-3 cargo plane full of loot. The passengers sit across rolls of spectacular Persian carpets. Only four years earlier, also in June, as a young field artillery commander, it took him months to reach Moscow on horseback. Now the return trip will take four hours.

Knappe had a good war, and he remembers the sunny times fondly. His father had been a naval gunnery officer in the First World War. At the *Kriegsschule* in Potsdam, he had graduated top of his class, and with other outstanding officers from three other *Kriegsschulen*, he had been introduced to Hitler at the Reich Chancellery in Berlin. All the top brass looked just as they did in the newsreels. For a 22-year-old officer this was quite a heady experience.

During those years, he was often told that he and other recruits belonged to a class of destiny. There were many impassioned speeches, and the army pay was splendid in addition to room and board. Near Karlsbad in Czechoslovakia, shortly after the Sudeten crisis in 1938, he had taken a motorcycle down a gravel road to drive from a restaurant in a small village to a larger town to get champagne and wine. He then woke up in Germany, north-east of Nuremberg. The nurse told him he had been unconscious for thirty-six hours and he had been wearing his steel helmet. No broken bones, no cuts. Not even a headache!

Knappe took part in the invasion of France and lost a dear friend by the name of Rehberg. 'What do you mean?' he had asked stupidly, like so many men of that generation. 'I thought you would want to know, since he was your friend.' Rehberg had been shot by a sniper.

At the Ourcq Canal near the Marne River, by which time Paris had been declared an open city, a bullet had gone through the back of his hand and exited through his wrist. The blood started oozing; the pain came later. Knappe also noticed a hole through the side of his jacket, one through his sleeve, and one through his map case. He silently counted his blessings. In June 1940, convalescing in Bonn, he was awarded the Iron Cross Second Class and the black *Verwundetenabzeichen* (3rd Class).

On 21 June 1941, artillery commanders were informed that Operation Barbarossa was about to begin. For months on end, Knappe and millions of other soldiers would be tormented not only by bullets and shells but also by lice, which were everywhere. Somewhere between Minsk and Smolensk, deep inside woods, where he thought that he and fifteen companions of his were safe, a chilling howl followed by artillery shells exploded 10 yards above him. He was unharmed and instantly yelled for medics.

The unfathomably vast size of Russia ever so slowly turned him into a fatalist. This merciless war of extermination, despite the occasional laughter, would sooner or later culminate in his death or mangling. The lack of warm felt boots and quilted uniforms decimated the morale of German troops. Frostbite took a heavy toll.

Near Peredelkino, a tank shell crashed through a corner of his hut and exploded, the room filling with smoke and the cries of wounded soldiers. Eight or ten Russian tanks had been able to slip past their defenses. Here Knappe lost another dear friend, and the news that his brother had died also reached him.

During the campaign in Italy in late 1943, Knappe received a telegram announcing the birth of his son. The same telegram announced that Leipzig was under bombardment and that his wife had left for Braunschweig. Taking a whole trunk of oranges and a turkey with him, Knappe managed to return to Germany to see his badly underweight 8-week-old newborn. He cursed the war for what it had done to his wife and his son.

Back in Italy, he established the defense line about 28 miles long in the half-circle to contain the American bridgeheads at Anzio. For some reason, the Americans did not attack.

In April 1944, following general staff training in three stages, people congratulated him as he joined the Kesselring staff, who commanded all German forces in the Mediterranean area. He was one of the few surviving graduates of the *Kriegsschule* class of 1938. His saving grace – and misfortune – was to end war as one of the few surviving officers to visit Hitler in the bunker.

— ✦ —

Located at 1400 Pennsylvania Avenue NW in the Social Security Building, the OWI is winding down its ingenious operations. People are showing up later to work. They leave earlier for the cocktail hour. But the war is far from over.

Now that the Nazis are defeated, the large-scale information and propaganda machine must turn its attention to the Pacific Theater. So far, the OWI has managed to create a distinct 'American lifestyle' account of the war, depicting freedom fighters and valiant women united in the war effort. The key, of course, is always to link the battlefront and civilian communities. 'Why are we doing this?' is now becoming 'What to show the world?'

The roster of talent at the OWI is extremely eclectic, a neat amalgam of West and East Coast characters: film directors, magazine publishers, playwrights, ethnomusicologists, historians, psychological warfare specialists, science-fiction writers, photographers, prep school alumni, and OSS operatives.

'Above and beyond the call of duty.' (NARA NAID: 513747 Local ID: 44-PA-300)

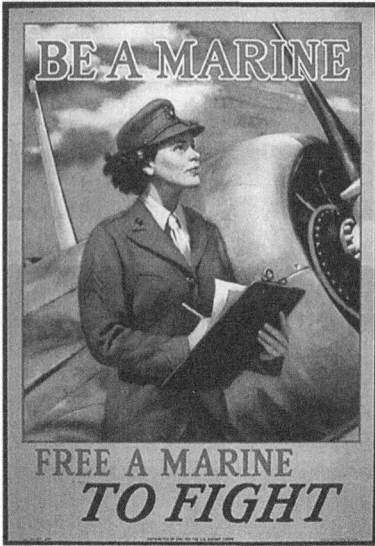

'Be a marine – free a
marine to fight.' (NARA
NAID: 513679 Local ID:
44-PA-236B)

— ✦ —

It's official: pay rates for Land Girls in New Zealand rise by
10 shillings for the 2,711 members placed on farms and working for the Women's Land Service. Perhaps the pay rise was
granted because of inordinately harsh winter conditions or
because victory is in sight. Yet the Land Girls continue to be
treated with suspicion and are tracked with binoculars. The
reaction from women is that 'you just have to get on with it'.

When British food supplies were at their lowest ebb,
the women in New Zealand managed to raise agricultural
output, despite lacking trucks and fertilizer. Particularly
irksome was the fact that rifles had been confiscated as
well, making it inordinately difficult to get rid of rabbits.
Still, many landowners considered the work unsuitable for
women and objected to women receiving the same wages as
men. *Thanks, girls, and Goodbye!*

July

On 1 July, *Vogue* magazine publishes a picture of Lee Miller taking a bath in Hitler's old flat in Munich. Back in Manhattan, Marlene Dietrich calls her agent in Hollywood to tell him that she wants to go on a second tour in Europe to entertain the troops. Well, there isn't enough money to pay for the taxi to take her back to the airport.

On a beautiful Sunday morning, Justice Robert Jackson motors up from London to meet an international law professor in Cambridge.

What would jazz be without Sarah Vaughan? She visits the Roxy every day because she is tired of touring the south. But will Count Basie notice her and hire her?

Churchill is out of power and the war is not even over! After years of waiting, Indira Gandhi is looking forward to a ten-day trek with her father, Jawaharlal Nehru.

On 1 July, American *Vogue* magazine publishes a picture of Lee Miller taking a bath in Hitler's Munich apartment. Her naked shoulders are visible, her face coquettish with a *soigné* appearance. Her right hand, enfolded in a washcloth, is placed over her left shoulder. Her face is turned to the camera, but her eyes are averted from the photographer. The army boots are at the bottom of the photograph, the fatigues

Lee Miller. (US Army Center of Military History, Wikimedia Commons)

folded on a nearby chair. On the right, a beautiful statuette emulates the gestures of the person in the bath.

The article describes portraits of Hitler tenderly autographed to Eva Braun. Part of the china is modern peasant and part is white porcelain dotted with pale-blue flowers. Lee takes a nap on Eva's bed. On the living-room table, designed to hold glasses and bottles for toasting, rests a large brass globe of the world.

— ◆ —

It rains on 13 July over LaGuardia Airport. Suffering from a jaw infection, Marlene Dietrich is momentarily back in the United States. It's her first furlough in nearly a year. She is dressed in her GI fatigues and battle boots. US Customs officials confiscate her pearl-handled revolver, a gift from General Patton.

Marlene Dietrich started her tour in the gaudy red and gold Algiers Opera House. Bad news: the master of ceremony on stage announced that the show was cancelled; an American officer had pulled rank for her services. Her services? Cancelled?

The men in uniform start booing and the clang of coins hitting the stage tells a long story. Then, somewhere, one hears, 'No, no. I'm here.' They watch her lanky body climb on stage. The perfectly stylized gestures of the body and hands. A face to make the gods envious, a face as smooth as a pebble in a mountain stream. She opens a small overnight case and withdraws evening slippers and an *evening* dress. She is every woman in the world rolled into one. The men are *screaming*. Is the mystery only a delusion? 'No, no, I'm here.'

Outside LaGuardia Airport, Marlene Dietrich invites the GIs to her suite at the St Regis Hotel, where they will be able to wash. She orders food and room service. After they finally leave, she calls up her agent in Hollywood. He reminds her there is no money to pay the taxi, no money to pay for the hotel suite, no cash advance, no money to entertain GIs, no cash advance in sight. She tells him she intends to go back, 'It's the only important thing I've ever done.'

— ✦ —

On 16 July, Harry Truman awakes in a villa near Potsdam. It's a ruined, yellowish, three-storey stucco villa on Lake Griebnitz. Officials mistakenly tell Truman that they are in the movie district of Berlin and the house used to belong to a prominent German filmmaker, the head of the Nazi movie industry. But the truth is more prosaic. The house belonged to a famous publisher, and when the Soviets arrived they ransacked his house, raped his daughters, and told him he had one hour to pack up and leave.

Truman is not keen on public functions, which are time-consuming and draining. The night before, Truman excused himself from a thirty-piece band playing a musical program and having to watch a movie shown in James Byrnes' quarters. Byrnes is one of his closest advisors, and an influential southern member of Congress. Truman prefers to retreat to his suite on the second floor of his new temporary home, where he can play poker with his closest circle of friends. During one of those poker conversations, Truman's chief of staff, Admiral Leahy, insists that the atomic bomb will never go off and he speaks as an expert in explosives, 'This is the biggest fool thing we have ever done'.

Winston Churchill visits Truman at around eleven in the morning. The British premier is full of flattery, a lot of hooey, and much soft soap, but the two seem to get along with a great deal of genuine mutual respect. That same afternoon, the whereabouts of Stalin are still unknown, so Truman decides to visit Berlin. In the First World War, he witnessed a lot of harm and damage as a captain in the Field Artillery. Riding in an open car to inspect the rubble of Berlin, Truman is shocked by the level of devastation, the stench of rotting bodies and wandering masses of German civilians.

On his way to the city center, the entire US 2nd Armored Division lines up along one side of the autobahn. The president reviews the troops in a half-track, driving past a mighty array of tanks, trucks, and Jeeps. It takes about twenty-two minutes to drive the length of the formation. We do not know the thoughts of those thousands of men lined up along the Autobahn, but they must be proud, and a great many wish that their closest friends were here on this day.

— ✦ —

On a bright Sunday morning, Justice Robert Jackson walks out of Claridge's Hotel in Mayfair, followed by his son, Bill, two secretaries, and a staff lawyer. A large military car waits for him. Appointed by President Truman to serve as US Chief Counsel for the prosecution of Nazi war criminals in Europe, Jackson is on the Supreme Court, though he never graduated from law school. FDR took an instant liking to him after being berated for the appalling conduct of the president's upstate New York Democrats. Jackson was the man behind the Lend–Lease deal with England.

The Allies have promised stern justice but there is no treaty, precedent, or custom to determine by what method justice should be done once Germany is defeated. The British and Soviets are both staunch in their opposition to a trial, even if they don't agree on how many Nazis should be shot – take the top Nazi criminals out and shoot them without warning one morning and then announce to the world that they are dead. Not only would an international trial be exceedingly long and elaborate, but it would also be open to misinterpretation by the public.

The mini-delegation glides out of Mayfair and the West End on its way north to Cambridge. In the car, Jackson shares his thoughts on the week ahead. He was in Germany, days earlier, when he learned that Churchill and the Conservatives had been voted out of power. The fear is that Labour will now complicate the wording of the charter of the International Military Tribunal (IMT). The French tend to side with the Soviets.

Jackson is going to Cambridge to hear the views of Professor Hersch Lauterpacht, a Polish exile and distinguished professor of international law, on indicting the SS and the Gestapo. But before business, Jackson invites the professor and his wife to a country inn. The party is then invited back to Cranmer Road to sit in the garden. The freshly cut lawn is as smooth as a tennis court. Lauterpacht's wife, Rachel, serves tea and coffee. A child wanders in from a neighboring garden.

Here's the problem: the Soviets may want to include only three crimes – aggression; atrocities against civilians in pursuance of the aggression; and violations of the laws of war. The Americans have proposed two additional crimes: waging an illegal war; and membership of an illegal organization. Jackson is adamant: he wants to ban aggressive wars of conquest. He is confronting 'the vanishing point of the law', where international law rules seem to disappear or become extremely hard to enforce due to a lack of a clear mechanism to punish perpetrators.

Lauterpacht grasps Jackson's lofty motives. Modern war spells the end of civilization. War itself must be illegal, and all wars begin with an aggression – so, ban aggression. Humanity will not survive another world war. The Cambridge professor thinks aloud: replace waging an illegal war with the suitably vague 'crimes against peace' to please the Soviets. Violations of the laws of war should come under 'war crimes'. Journalists will like it. If Russians and Americans cannot agree on atrocities against civilians in pursuance of the aggression, why not simply call them 'crimes against humanity'? The public will understand. A similar expression was used to condemn horrific Turkish policies against Armenians back in 1915. The key is to create separate titles so that journalists can grasp the novelty of proceedings.

— ✦ —

Count Basie looks tired. His features are drawn. He is auditioning new vocalists before the evening show, Thelma Carpenter having left the band. 'I'll play for you,' Sarah Vaughan says in a gentle voice. 'You just lie over there and listen and let me play,' she offers again.

'Well, if you don't really mind.' After listening to two or three applicants, he needs to relax before the evening's next set.

Basie and his band have an extended engagement at the Roxie Theater and Sarah Vaughan visits every day, spending a lot of time backstage. They call her 'Sassie' by now. Every now and then, he enquires about her tour in the South with Erskine Hawkins and 'Tuxedo Junction', one of the most popular songs of the Second World War.

'Yeah, one girl and sixteen guys; what the hell? What can I say.'

Resting on the couch, he asks about her tour in the South. Church-bred Vaughan is reluctant to dwell on the heat, the overcrowded trains, the seedy world of drug addicts, pushers, hustlers. Checking for vermin feces, ground glass and other surprises when buying a sandwich. They once hit twenty-five bases in twenty-eight days. The axle-grease fried chicken. The strict caste system. Time to move on.

Vaughan offers feedback after every applicant. As he auditions other singers, Count Basie has no idea that he has one of the greatest vocalists in the same room, and Vaughan doesn't let on.

This will go on for a couple of weeks. She will come over every day and play for him, so all he has to do is lie down between the shows and listen. She comes every goddamn day, playing the piano, so he can audition other singers.

— ✦ —

Early to bed is one in the morning for Winston Churchill. Shortly before dawn, he is awakened with a sharp stab of physical pain. The realization that the Tories are down and out. Beaverbrook's rosy predictions all wrong.

Churchill sinks back into peaceful sleep and gets up at nine. He is in his bath when Captain Pim requests his presence in the map room. The lists of constituencies are waiting for him. Attired in his siren suit, as though he is getting ready for an air-raid alarm, Churchill learns that he keeps his seat. So does Foreign Secretary Anthony Eden. But Britain's wartime Minister for Information Brendan Bracken lost his seat. Expert on anti-aircraft warfare Duncan Sandys, his protégé Harold Macmillan, and his son Randolph are also out.

Mary tells her diary that lunch takes place in Stygian gloom. Sarah looks beautiful but distressed. This is a terrible, terrible blow.

Clementine describes the defeat as a blessing in disguise.

'Well, at this moment it's certainly *very* well disguised.'

In the afternoon, Churchill retires to draft a concession statement to be sent to the BBC. At six in the evening, he orders drinks and cigars to be brought to the map-room staff. Then he takes leave for a seven o'clock appointment with King George at Buckingham Palace. Make sure the streets are very quiet.

Cold rain. Buckingham within sight. Churchill is pleased to see that the Mall is deserted. No feverish throngs clinging to the railings, no Labour voters gathered to celebrate the end of his stewardship. Merely the changing of the guard.

The king tactfully tells his former prime minister that the people were very ungrateful after the way they had been led in war. On his way back to dinner at No. 10 Downing Street, Churchill is reminded of a letter from Sarah following his 'Gestapo' speech. He can't help it; his mind is on tragic changes in Eastern Europe.

Sarah had praised his speech but also reminded him of the virtues of wartime socialism: 'The children of this country have been so well fed – what milk there was, was shared equally.' Well, socialism is interwoven with totalitarianism and the abject worship of the state. Vast bureaucracies of civil servants, no longer servants and no longer civil. 'Don't think I am a rebel.' His daughter had suggested a housing program, which he had included in his next electoral speech.

Churchill broods over the fourteen arrested Polish political leaders, the Soviet forces controlling a broad swathe of land

A changing of the guard. From left to right, newly elected British Prime Minister Clement Attlee, President Harry S. Truman, and Soviet Prime Minister Joseph Stalin at the Potsdam Conference. (US Army Signal Corps, Harry S. Truman Library & Museum, NARA 348307597)

Former First Lady Eleanor Roosevelt and General Dwight D. Eisenhower visiting Franklin D. Roosevelt's Grave, Hyde Park, New York. (Franklin D. Roosevelt Presidential Library 46-8-1(3))

in central Germany and Czechoslovakia. Human observers are incensed to see this world-class leader thrown out of power. Maybe other good things will happen to him. This is a chance for him to express his gratitude. The setback will force him to write a story of the war. He will also be able to paint, and talk to his cat and feed the ducks, don't you think?

He stood up against Hitler. Is that not enough? Back and forth between humans and angels. He could have died on his way to Malta. Now, he will be able to retire on the French Riviera.

Dinner is fortunately less gloomy than lunch. Maria, Diana, and Sarah are all present. Churchill's brother, Uncle Jack, has joined 'the party of loss and defeat', together with Bracken. Remarkably, Anthony Eden is also on hand. Just five days earlier, he had learned that his son, RAF Pilot Officer Simon Eden, had been killed in Burma.

At 9 p.m., Churchill's words of departure are broadcast to the nation:

> I regret that I have not been permitted to finish the work against Japan ... It only remains for me to express to the British people, for whom I have acted in these perilous years, my profound gratitude for the unflinching, unswerving support which they have given me during my task, and for the many expressions of kindness they have shown towards their servant.

— ✦ —

It was once a staging post on the Silk Road, connecting Kashmir and Tibet. Sonamarg, which means 'Meadow Gold', is a popular hill station, an upper-class hiking destination. It resembles Swiss alpine meadows in the summer with its yellow-button flowers, scenic lakes, and charming glaciers.

Indira Gandhi, the only child of Jawaharlal Nehru and Kamala Nehru, is looking forward to a ten-day trek with her father. He wrote to her that he would clear his crowded schedule. She hasn't enjoyed his company in more than two and half years.

She decides to leave her 1-year-old son, Rajiv, with her aunt and wonders whether her health, lacking oxygen, will betray her at the wrong moment. Since early childhood she has been plagued by physical and mental problems and just now, in June, during the relentless mid-monsoon rains, she caught a severe cold, which developed into bronchitis.

The ten-day trek will remain one of Indira's most-cherished memories. Ever so slowly, as they camp by mountain streams, the carefree beauty envelops her like a warm blanket. Encircled by majestic snow-filled ranges, she and her father observe pale flowers forging a path, forcing their way out from under boulders of icy streams – a metaphor for the upcoming fate of India. They cross mountain meadows boasting a near infinite number of wildflowers, just like India. They bathe in the waters of Gangabal Lake. They travel about 100 miles at altitudes ranging from 9,000 to 14,000ft. A false step and you would plummet 400ft below, before even the people ahead of you notice anything.

Indira has never been able to distinguish her own inner turmoil from the larger social and political canvas. Her early life was deeply intertwined with the political and social upheaval of India's struggle for independence. Or maybe the expectations were too high.

Her childhood years were plagued by loneliness and incessant turmoil. Her father's absence and her mother's illness affected her in more ways than one. After individual tutoring at home, they sent her to a boarding school, the École Nouvelle in Switzerland. At Somerville College, Oxford, she joined the Indian League. There she also met Feroze Gandhi, a fellow student, and the two were married in 1942, despite opposition from her family. The early years of marriage had been challenging because of their imprisonment in separate jails.

During this bucolic journey, her father wants to strengthen the Nehru political dynasty. She herself wants to refine her political outlook and carve out her own path to leadership. Not least, Mahatma Gandhi, who was released in 1944, needs special medical attention.

When Nehru enquires about her own personal challenges, Indira is cautious. There is no reason to recall the childhood illnesses, the frequent colds, the fevers. Or how in her late teens she was diagnosed with pleurisy, which in the late 1930s turned into tuberculosis and periods in Swiss sanatoriums. Malaria further weakened her, but who hasn't had malaria in India?

The separation from her husband during their imprisonment had been hard, but also a source of inner strength and resolve. All told, her most-significant emotional and physical challenge had happened shortly after her release when news of the devastating famine in Bengal appeared in the newspapers. The monsoon storms had made things worse or had intertwined the personal and the national, the sense of death by starvation for millions.

To be sure, her father's soothing words from prison had sustained her and here they were now, surviving together across dangerous passes. Yes, Jawaharlal concedes, her letters alarmed him. He had responded from prison, trying to lift her spirits: 'Everything changes', new seeds would germinate. He had also reminded her of Beethoven's resolve when stricken by deafness, 'I shall seize fate by the throat; it shall never wholly overcome me.'

August

A billionth of a second. On 6 August, a B-29 Superfortress named *Enola Gay* releases an atomic bomb over Hiroshima. Reluctant to interrupt his nap, Jackson Pollock hears the garbled news on a secluded beach on Long Island. Emperor Hirohito addresses the nation to announce a ceasefire, and Japanese officers write haikus and commit *seppuku*.

In south-eastern Europe, bloody purges are under way. On 12 August in Belgrade, Marshall Josip Broz Tito gives a press conference to reassure foreign correspondents.

It's Victory in the Pacific Day! In the city of Perth, men and women dance in the streets while others barricade themselves in a hotel to avoid a catastrophic crush on the bar. '*C'est pas croyable!*'

The mine workers at Shinkolobwe in the Belgian Congo wonder how that leaden, yellowish cake they dug up created such havoc over Japan. On 26 August, Frida Kahlo completes *Without Hope*. Is this really the case?

It takes some convincing for Mao to board the US four-engine C-47 to travel to Chongqing. Maria Klimoff makes her way to Prague to obtain an exit visa to the American zone of occupation.

1945

It's a sunny Monday morning in early August. No school. Vast, beautiful, cloudless skies. At seven o'clock the temperature is already 80 degrees. The city seems to be so happy that its finger-shaped deltas stretch out and sparkle with abandonment. Shimmering leaves, which many elderly people notice, are basking in the reflected light.

A first red-alert warning of an enemy plane overhead blared at 12.35 a.m. that night and was canceled at 2.10 a.m. At 7.09 a.m., a second air-raid warning, this time a yellow alert, warned of enemy planes approaching, but the all-clear sounded at 7.31 a.m.

Another yellow alert will be typed up shortly after eight o'clock, along the same, established procedural lines: 'Chugokoyu District Army Information at 8.13: three enemy Superfortresses proceeding westward over Saijo area. Strict precautions should be taken.'

The children are waking up, sleepy and yawning. Today, they will again proudly wear their head bands to show their devotion to the emperor. Today, they will clear fire lanes or sit down at long communal tables to build parts of tanks, shells, or aircraft engines. Soldiers stripped to their waist are doing morning calisthenics. Two lovers who climbed over a fence to spend the night holding hands in the grass of a public park have taken leave of one another.

Miss Horibe arrives early at her elementary school, having taken an early streetcar to make time for unreliable commuting schedules. Eighteen-year-old Motoji Maeoka grabs a green blanket to momentarily lie down for a rest. Eizo Nomura, a clerk for the Fuel Distribution and Control Co-operative, goes into the basement to retrieve a document for his chief. Taeko Teramae, a temporary switchboard operator at the telephone exchange, begins her 8.15 a.m. shift.

Mrs Aoyama, whose house leans against a Buddhist temple, is pleased with the thought that she sent her son Nenkai away to school a half-hour earlier than usual. Akiko Takakura and her friend Asami, both workers at the Sumitomo Bank, joke about the big clock atop the Hiroshima University Tower which had stopped three days earlier, frozen seemingly forever at 8.15. Shigeyoshi Morimoto, one of Japan's top champion kite-makers, has an idea. Toshihiko Matsuda is bending down in his garden to pick up a fruit or a leaf.

Rumiko Kirihara's family has been scheduled for a group portrait in the sunny garden, a final reunion as more family members are drafted, but the photographer is late. Mrs Teruoko Konoto is watching her son play from the second-storey window of her riverside home. Not far from the Hiroshima Dome, Nobuo Tetsutani hears the laughter of 3-year-old Shin and his friend, Kimi, as they ride together on a tricycle painted dark red.

Etsuko Juramoto is a fifth-grader who had already stayed home for three days with a recurrent stomachache. She did not want to go to school again, insisting that something was about to happen and she did not want her mother to be lonely. 'Well then,' Etsuko's mother says, 'we'll die together when we die.' Sumi Kumamoto watches her adored child walking toward the National Elementary School wearing 'her Sunday best'. Teacher Arai is hanging the best examples of delicate calligraphy in India ink on rice paper in the window – alone in her schoolroom.

North of the city, Dr Shuntaro Hida has just woken up with a massive hangover. The night before, he had entertained and lodged visitors from Manchuria in the center of town. An elderly terrified farmer had woken him in middle of the night to take a look at his granddaughter all the way up in Hesaka.

Satoshi Nakamura, a reporter for Donei, the government news agency, is having breakfast at a friend's house, 8 miles to the west of the city. Tsutomu Yamagushi has been basking in the warmth of a potato field alongside a woman dressed in a black *monpe*. Isao Kita, the chief military weather forecaster for the District Bureau from the weather station has a grandstand view looking north across the city.

Is it a chemist's nightmare? No, not exactly. Is it a physicist's nightmare? You might call it that. Do your jobs. Obey your orders. Don't cut corners or take chances. Watches are synchronized on Saipan Island at 12.15 p.m. The weather crews will transmit their report and then Paul Tibbets will decide. 'Almighty Father, we pray Thee to be with those who brave the heights of Thy heaven and who carry the battle to our enemies. Guard and protect them. Bring this war to a rapid end.'

A scrum of photographers crowd the plane's nose wheel. An MGM stage with Klieg lights and scores of cameras and photographers flashing their bulbs, all but the end of deepest secrecy.

Time to pressurize the cabin. The plane begins the long climb to reach its operational bombing altitude. *Enola Gay* is preceded by three weather planes and followed by two more airplanes packed with measuring instruments and state-of-the-art cameras.

Eight large ships are in view in the harbor. It's all yours.

They are almost 6 miles above sea level and approaching their target at a ground speed of 285mph. The aiming point – the center of a bridge – appears in the crosshairs of his sight. He yells out that he has it and starts the automatic process that will release the bomb in sixty seconds. They have practiced this for eleven months, so the process is almost anti-climactic.

Forty-five seconds later, the radio tone begins signifying that the bomb will drop in exactly fifteen seconds. The men on *Enola Gay*, *Great Artiste*, and *No. 91* hear the continuous radio tone and pull down their goggles. They are special Polaroid glasses, shaped like welders' goggles. The lenses have quinine crystals to keep out all but purple light.

Hundreds of miles away, *Jabbit III*, *Straight Flush*, and *Full House*, flying home to Tinian, pick up the tone on their radios and know the sequence. Even farther away, on Iwo Jima, Captain McKnight, sitting in the cockpit of *Top Secret*, hears it on his radio.

Fifteen seconds. The airplane's pneumatically operated bomb-bay doors spring open. 'Bombs away!' shouts Ferebee. Five tons lighter, the plane jumps up. The bomb falls broadside at first and then the tail fins catch the rarefied air for a nose-first dive.

The instant 'Little Boy No. 1' tumbles out to leave the bay, the electrical contact and the radio tone stop. At that exact moment, *Great Artiste*'s bombardier hits the switch that opens the bomb-bay doors in his plane. He releases three instrument packages, which are soon swinging on their individual para-chutes, floating earthward toward the T-shaped bridge.

Enola Gay lurches up dramatically and enters a 60-degree dive and 158-degree right turn. This is the moment the two planes go into their well-honed, parallel maneuvers, *Enola Gay* taking a sharp dive to the right, and *Great Artiste*, a matching turn to the left. The bomb is headed for the Aioi Bridge, and one can see the seven fingers branching off the Ota River, stretched out like a familiar hand. Radio silence was broken a few minutes ago.

Members of the crew are mentally adding each elapsed second. At the count of thirty-five, Tibbets pulls his goggles over his eyes as instructed, but unable to see through them, throws them to the floor. He wonders whether the 'gadget' will really work. 'See anything yet, Bob?' Tibbets asks Caron on the intercom.

'No, sir,' replies the tail gunner.

At forty-three, Jeppson stops counting. 'It's a dud,' he thinks.

A billionth of a second. In a few hours, in a few days, words such as 'atomic' and 'hypocenter' will enter the English language – will enter every language. News dispatches will display visual evidence and bizarre radiating circles. Anecdotes will surface about survivors dragging themselves to Nagasaki for safety. Historians will next emphasize the novelty, the teamwork, and the original desire to drop the atomic bomb over Nazi Germany. Would there have been a way to subdue the atavistic tendencies, the efficient intelligence, the uprightness of the participants?

— ◆ —

When the strange, garbled news that a bomb has been dropped somewhere over Japan comes, Jackson Pollock is lying on a secluded beach on the eastern tip of Long Island. He doesn't even open his eyes. He is spending an idyllic summer at a beachside shack. The light is that of a vast, virgin continent.

Jackson Pollock accepted an invitation from the Kadish family. Reuben Kadish is a young sculptor and one of Jackson's closest friends. Both are perennially short of funds and whatever they have is shared. Reuben was offered a shack at the far edge of Long Island, and he accepted, next inviting Jackson and his partner.

Reuben's minuscule guest house sits at the edge of Gardiners Bay. He and his wife have two children, three bikes, and a dog. You can see Accabonac to the west, and to the east, you feel the soft breeze from the ocean beyond. Guests sleep on the porch. With no electricity, a leaky roof, and hand-pumped water, the sublet is admittedly tiny and shabby, but what's the worry? No one is spending any time indoors.

In the morning, they wade through the chilly water in search of clams through the clouds of mud. Later in the day, they climb into a rowboat to catch some fish for dinner. When they run out of supplies, they trek on their bicycles past potato fields to the Amagansett general store, trying to balance as much beer as possible on the rack.

'Little Boy' atomic bomb in its concrete pit, August 1945. (NARA NAID: 519394 Local ID: 77-BT-115)

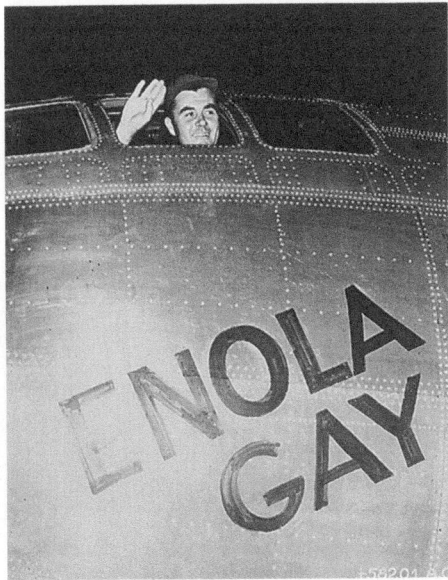

Colonel Paul W. Tibbets Jr waves from his cockpit before take-off, 6 August 1945. (NARA NAID: 535737 Local ID: 208-LU-13H(5))

Enola Gay returns home after the atomic bombing of Hiroshima. (NARA NAID: 76048622 Local ID: 77-BT-90)

Hiroshima Prefectural Industrial Promotion Hall after it was destroyed by the atomic bomb. (NARA NAID: 350382730 Local ID: 2023-507)

— ✦ —

The text of the emperor's broadcast has already been released to the Domei news agency with instructions to withhold it until the actual broadcast at noon on 15 August. Just after midnight, the NHK television crew packs up its gear and places the records of the emperor's voice into metal cases in two cotton bags. Then the siren wails, announcing a B-29 raid over Tokyo.

The regimental commanders (wrongly) believe they are obeying General Mori's orders. Entering the sacred compound, the Imperial Guards cut the palace's telephone lines. Next, the troops break into the building. A chamberlain by the name of Tokugawa is severely beaten up for protesting the disturbance. Meanwhile, some of Hirohito's closest advisors hide in the palace bank vault.

The rebels rush in every direction, desperate to capture the emperor's surrender speech. The recording must be in the palace. 'Where is it?'

But no one inside the palace has any idea where the announcement might be. In fact, a junior chamberlain has put the records in a small safe inside one of the palace offices. He couldn't risk sending them to the NHK building in the middle of an air raid.

The emperor is only now becoming aware of his predicament. He is driven a short distance to the Imperial air-raid shelter. He is underweight and dizzy with fatigue. A handful of chamberlains gather at the entrance. In accordance with his divine status, the emperor gives the appearance of sleeping undisturbed. Every now and then, he overhears the voices of the chamberlains nearby and begins to understand his true predicament.

At the palace, the ringleader, NCOs and rebel soldiers ransack the palace but come up empty-handed. They are running out of time. Major Kenji Hatanaka's plot is on the verge of failing, but he is not ready to give up.

Driving at full speed on his motorcycle to the NHK building, he demands admittance. There he tells technicians that he intends to go on air. 'No broadcast during an alert,' says the announcer on duty. He is none other than Morio Tateno, who spoke into the microphone on 8 December 1941, announcing the start of the war. Tateno's authority is such that Hatanaka retreats.

A telephone call. Someone is demanding to speak to Major Hatanaka. He straightens up and says, 'Yes, sir' several times. As he sets the phone down in the cradle, he mutters, 'It's all over.'

At regular intervals, NHK announces that a broadcast of the highest importance is to be made. Meanwhile, tons of papers are thrown of out ministry windows. In the streets below, tall bonfires burn. It's time to destroy the evidence of crimes.

— ◆ —

Elsewhere in Japan, the mood is subdued. People can't sleep. Navy and army soldiers and auxiliary troops are armed to the teeth. The indoctrinated soldiers were looking forward to an honorable death in the final battle for mainland Japan. They discuss among themselves last-ditch, cheat-the-enemy tactics to duck shameful surrender. Pilots vaguely dream of sinking a US aircraft carrier.

Officers can't bear the thought that the emperor is conceding. They feel guilty for losing the war. They pen a posthumous message making manifest the glory of Japan's national polity. Many contemplate *seppuku*, plunging short samurai swords into their bellies, to prove the nobility of their spirit.

The officers discuss politics. What about the emperor and the cessation of hostilities? General Anami jokes with his brother-in-law, Lieutenant Colonel Takeshita. Takeshita can't help but admire how this true Samurai prepares for death. Anami's handwriting on the parchment is stylish and sophisticated:

> After tasting the profound benevolence of the emperor,
> I have no words to speak.

On another piece of paper, he records a second epigram:

> For my supreme crime, I beg forgiveness through this
> act of death.

— ◆ —

On 11 August, a pregnant and anxious Carol Zens Kellam writes a letter to her husband, John Kellam, who happens to be behind bars. She is a Quaker woman sharing her thoughts with the future father of her child and expecting imminent news of the end of the war. Her husband is serving a five-year prison sentence for violating the Selective Training and Service Act. She confides that, as yet, there are no signs of Junior's debut and that even though she hopes for news of victory any minute now, she will not hail 'victory' because the war has been horribly costly. As for their own imminent future, there is no saying, for no one knows 'how vindictive our government is'.

— ◆ —

It is a region famous for its gifts of buckets full of eyeballs. On 12 August in Belgrade, speaking at a reception for foreign correspondents, the Yugoslav premier, Marshal Tito, denies that his country is on the road to a Communist regime or that he is planning one. His total self-confidence is hard to miss. Once a famished guerrilla fighter, Tito behaves now like an elegant statesman and diplomat. Asked about his program of radical reforms, Tito responds that what we are doing serves the country's interests and corresponds to our type of democracy. Tito never confides his intentions or ambitions even to his closest advisors, so perhaps the foreign journalists should not expect too much from this press conference.

Once a locksmith, then a steelworker, Tito had been conscripted into the Habsburg Army during the First World War. Sergeant Major Broz had been stabbed in the back below his left arm with a long two-pronged lance that just missed his heart, but it was still a serious wound. He had lost consciousness. Sent to a hospital, he developed pneumonia and caught typhus. Unconscious with high fever, a nurse had tied a red ribbon to his bed, intimating that he should be left to die. But 'Broz' had somehow recovered, then joined the Bolshevik forces.

Back in Belgrade, he organized May Day demonstrations and strikes, with predictable results. In the spring of 1934, he was released from prison after 2,046 days.

Success for carrying out underground missions in Vienna and Ljubljana earned him a promotion in Moscow as CPY representative of the Comintern in the mid-1930s. He had stayed at the famous Hotel Lux, where knocks on the door at night and disappearances of exiled Party cadres were routine.

Back home during the war, he had begun the Long March in 1942, bringing the badly wounded across freezing mountain passes. Hitler, over time, became obsessed with Tito, 'Remember, [Field Marshal] von Weichs, Tito must be captured alive … And he must be brought here without anyone knowing it.' Some 900 German troops, six glider groups, and three parachute groups had participated in a failed airborne assault to arrest the barbaric Balkans resistance fighter.

While he seems so self-assured now, pacing the stage, with his blue eyes and his dominant but gentle personality, Tito's deep inner life is in turmoil. Many of his closest wartime companions did not survive the war. Out of the 12,000 members of the Communist Party of Yugoslavia who were alive in 1941, 9,000 were killed.

His love life is in shambles. In 1918, he had met the 14-year-old Pelagija (Polka) Denisovna Belousova from Omsk and he had married her the following year. They had lost first a baby boy at birth and then, in 1923, a 2-year-old girl. During his imprisonment in the early 1930s, his wife returned to Russia and fell in love with another man, leaving their son, Žarko, to grow up in institutions. Pelagija later vanished in the Gulag archipelago.

Next, Tito had fallen in love with the intellectuals Lucia Bauer and Herta Haas. The latter had given birth to their son Mišo the day after they were separated early in the war. Later released during a dicey prisoner exchange, Herta walked in on Tito and his new lover, the stunning if ever-quarrelsome Zdenka, thirty years Tito's junior. Herta kept her distance and found herself a legal husband.

No one knows when Zdenka died of tuberculosis, except that Tito buried her in the White Palace Garden. After that, with trigger-happy security guards, Tito found it hard to bring a woman unnoticed into his bedroom.

At the end of his press conference, Tito insists that private property is respected here. We have nationalized only properties belonging to enemies and traitors, he says. A day will come when Tito will be condemned for killing the 23,000 refugees handed over to him from Trieste and Austria by Britain in late May. But right now, the Serbians condemn him for killing so few.

— ✦ —

A group of unidentified civilian men and women celebrating in the streets of Perth on Victory in the Pacific (VP) Day. (Australian War Memorial AWM2018.641.1)

Two Australian men celebrate with a drink on VP Day in Perth. (Australian War Memorial AWM2018.641.3)

Early in the morning on Victory in the Pacific Day in the city of Perth, all the whistles start blowing, as do the horns, with cars tearing around everywhere. In the Old Metropole Hotel, free drinks are handed out. Betty Atkinson is standing and singing on a table and all the doors have been locked to prevent a catastrophic crush. There is no choice but to go with the mob outside through the inner-city streets. A baby is snatched playfully from a pram, hoisted aloft on friendly shoulders, and carried down the street, its mother in anxious pursuit.

— ◆ —

When the mine workers at Shinkolobwe find out that their uranium helped to build the atomic bomb, they are positively shocked. The Congolese vaguely knew that *les Américains* had bought supplies at breakneck speed. The 'yellow cake' had first been dispatched by train from Kolwezi to Lobito in Angola. Later, for unknown reasons, a much more complicated route had transported the strategic ore by railhead to Port-Francqui and from there by barge up the Kasai River, where it joins the Congo River to Leopoldville. From there it went by rail to Matadi, where it was transferred to speed boats.

C'est fini. The managers of the Union Minière should be pleased to have played such a discreet but decisive role in the war effort, supplying strategic metals to the insatiable American war industry. Yet there is also a nagging fear that they might soon run out of the precious ore. And what to make of the new attitude among miners and workers, a spirit of antipathy and defiance, as though they're entitled to 'native' rights. The Sûreté d'État is investigating the matter of syndicalism and trade unionism, putting together a list of Bolshevist agitators. When in doubt, gather the ringleaders on a soccer pitch, and the Force Publique will shoot the rowdiest Congolese, point-blank.

— ✦ —

In Mexico City, Frida Kahlo completes *Sin Esperanza* (*Without Hope*) on 26 August 1945. The title says it all. Can the pain get any worse? In the painting, she is weeping in bed. Her head is propped up on a pillow. Between her lips, she holds what looks like a wooden contraption – an oversized membranous funnel that is force-feeding her with dead matter as part of her treatment. A cornucopia of gore – a pig, brains, turkey, chicken, beef, sausage, fish. Her own visage is meticulously painted. The unnatural feeding is nightmarish. The color palette is warm earth colors and muted hues, with a barren desert in the background.

Blending surrealism and realism, *Sin Esperanza* candidly depicts a woman's suffering while also asserting bodily autonomy. Kahlo has managed to convert her deepest suffering into timeless art. She painted this work of art as an ironic response to the cheerful bedside manner of her doctor announcing, 'Now you can eat anything!' In fact, she is being tube fed every two hours. A funnel of horror.

Indeed, the painting implies that the gore might be gushing in the opposite direction, nausea being the ruling sensation. Art is only one of Frida Kahlo's many coping mechanisms. She is fully aware that her naked body is prey to a variety of corsets, microbes and, yes, eternal forces. In true Aztec fashion, her latest painting incorporates the simultaneous presence of the sun and moon, the sadness of all creation.

Her body's misadventures are also recorded in a playful diary filled with random thoughts, poetry, and sketches in the margin. She collects silver rings and embroidered dresses, endlessly fascinated by Mexican folk tradition, more specifically, textile skills sustained by armies of invisible women in indigenous communities.

She has an inner circle of friends, lovers, philanthropists, and pen pals. Some visitors know that she likes to receive dolls as presents and she likes to assemble Pre-Columbian jade beads with metal *milagros* to keep Mayan art alive. Wit and humor, as well as alcohol and painkillers, every so often are defiantly propped up to contain the relentless assaults on her body. Caza Azul, her sanctuary in Coyoacán, is filled with art. Acts of defiance!

— ◆ —

It takes some convincing for Mao to board the four-engine C-47 to travel to Chongqing. US Ambassador Patrick J. Hurley has to give him his word that he will be under his protection during negotiations with Chiang Kai-shek. This is Mao's first flight. An inveterate smoker, he makes genuine efforts to exhale slowly.

Ambassador Hurley talks at length on the state of the world while Zhou Enlai and Mao give the impression of listening closely. The American's nickname is 'Clown'. Since the summer, Mao is in total control of the Party. Nevertheless, he is in a tight corner insofar as his sworn enemy Chiang Kai-shek has cast-iron American support. And Stalin's aloof neutrality is nerve-racking. The latter derided the Chinese as 'margarine Communists'.

On the flight to Chongqing, he pens a poem, while the smooth and sophisticated Zhou keeps nodding and smiling as though every word the ambassador says is of paramount importance. Zhou hopes Mao will stick to the script and sign a memorandum of understanding. In the last few weeks, he went to work on his boss – we have a very difficult hand to play; it's imperative to not alienate the US 'middle forces'; if negotiations break down, the Americans will blame Communist intransigence and opt for a military solution that will favor our sworn enemy. Tactical flexibility is paramount. Zhou encourages Mao to only use the word 'democracy'.

Mao Zedong travelled from the city of Yan'an (Shaanxi province) to Chongqing. (Wikimedia Commons)

We were never Communists but 'agrarian socialists'. Please, no 'adventurism' or other 'left-wing infantilism', if we can avoid it. Our aim is not Soviet-style communism, but a mixed economy, a 'new democracy' platform.

Since 1927, Mao had been treated as a bandit in the gen-eralissimo's territory. It might be thought that Ambassador Hurley is unreasonable in his bid to see the two chief warlords reach a pragmatic agreement, but they have done so in the past. It's true that Chiang presently enjoys remarkable popu-larity in the United States for his valiant wartime resistance to Japanese invaders and Madame Chiang Kai-shek's artful portrayal of Chinese sacrifice. The Nationalists did try hard to limit disruption and depredations at the hands of Japanese troops, while Mao's revolutionary troops avoided clashes with the occupying powers.

It is clear that in the past, the two bitter rivals signed agree-ments with both local warlords and with each other. The first interim peace agreement between Chiang and Mao lasted from 1921 to 1927, and the second truce lasted from 1937 until very recently. During the Japanese occupation, the two rival teams had come together to create a 'united front' against Japan. In a way, the Japanese invasion had been a gift from heaven for Mao, because by 1935, the Nationalists had secured the almost total annihilation of the Communists, shattering and demoralizing Mao's ragtag army. Now, however, the shoe is on the other foot: Chiang's troops are full of apathy and despair.

Would the two fraternal twins ever come to an understanding or are they irreducible enemies? The savage battles in the past raged for a reason. The Nationalists only care for city centers, railway lines, coal mines, and trading ports. Urban centers were all they worried about, places where money changes hands, where polite staff in well-lit restaurants greet you at the door. The Communists care only for peasant support. They are Marxists only to the extent that they cling to a binary interpretation of history and because they are drawn to the destitute masses.

As the airplane begins its descent, Mao is aware that there is no reason to alienate the growing American presence just now. Hurley himself is a fierce anti-communist. He doesn't want a US counter-intervention in a country as immense as China, yet he is too committed to the Nationalists, too close to Chiang. He envisions a coalition government, one completely dominated by Chiang, which is unacceptable to the Communists. The generalissimo, in turn, has not the slightest desire to order a ceasefire or agree to an alliance with the Communist rebels. But he is ostensibly unwilling to defy Hurley for he needs American fuel, spare parts, cash, ammunition.

A scrum of photographers and journalists surround the lumbering American airplane. Mao exits in the company of the immaculately groomed Hurley, who waves at the crowds. With his bow tie, double-breasted suit, and genial manner, the State Department official is the epitome of elegance. Mao looks bohemian. He seems silent, self-effacing, modest. Zhou's dress is worn and faded.

Let's get on with it. In the next six weeks, Chiang and Mao will meet face to face four times. They will approve a memorandum of understanding in which they both promise resolutely to avoid a civil war.

— ✦ —

Official relations between the US and the Soviet Union are still fairly cordial. In any case, the American military mission in Prague is still open to the public and it seems that Maria Klimoff might have no trouble gaining access. With the help of a dictionary, she has cobbled together a dozen sentences in English, starting with the answer to the first question, 'How can I help you?' She dressed up for the occasion, aware that her halting English might not carry the day. She has made mental notes in her head: remain calm and persuasive.

She proceeds to lay out her request in hesitant sentences to the military person on duty. He listens to her coldly and responds with a set phrase to the effect that the mission could not involve itself in matters of this sort. Maria Klimoff starts to sob. The last hope of getting an exit or transit visa seems to have been extinguished.

Maria Klimoff belongs to the large Russian Old Believer community in Latvia. The family's wartime odyssey began in Riga. When Latvia was absorbed by the Soviet Union in June 1940 as a result of the notorious Molotov–Ribbentrop Pact, she and her husband started to make every effort to get out of the bloodlands between East and West. When the Red Army occupied the country, her husband lost his job as a museum employee. He is a professional artist, a 1929 graduate of the

Latvian Academy of Art. The Klimoffs have two young children, and they live with a grandmother.

At some point in the spring of 1944, her husband had been invited to Prague to serve as an icon restorer in the Kondakov Institute. This is a prestigious research institute dedicated to the study of medieval culture, primarily involving Russia and Byzantium. They had a large supply of icons, many of them brought out of Russia by the Germans. Eugene Klimoff had been involved in both painting and restoring icons in Riga.

The job offer was thereupon accepted, and her husband had left for Czechoslovakia. The rest of the family had followed weeks later, first by boat to a Polish haven, then by train to a tiny apartment in Saaz, a Sudetenland town some 50km west of Prague. Her husband stayed with friends in Prague and came to see the family in Saaz only occasionally because of the difficulty of getting wartime travel permits.

All is probably lost. As Maria Klimoff dabs her eyes, alerted by sobbing, a door to an inner office opens and a higher-ranking officer emerges. 'What is the problem, madam?' he asks. It could have been, 'What seems to be the problem, Madam?' or any other expression, but the man is courteous. He listens to her halting, tear-filled explanations with sympathy. Then he gives her his calling card. He advises her to show his card to a representative of Caritas, the Catholic charitable organization that would provide the actual departure permits. Passing the man's card must be a prearranged signal, for the needed permits will be issued.

September

Ho Chi Minh declares Vietnam's independence. The sun bursts through at the ceremony aboard USS *Missouri* in Tokyo Bay, with General Douglas MacArthur accepting the Japanese surrender.

At the Rangoon Orient Club, a young Burman leader by the name of Aung Sang is invited to the table of Lord Louis Mountbatten. Meanwhile, Lady Edwina Mountbatten tours prisoner-of-war camps and unexpectedly stumbles upon an emaciated cousin.

In Nuremberg, hundreds of German laborers are put to work to build the International Military Tribunal (IMT) courthouse and an adjoining prison. Two young fathers – Walter Sisulu and Nelson Mandela – stand outside their home in Soweto, cradling their babies. In Paris, spectators flock to Camus' new play, *Caligula*. In Greenwich village, Dawn Powell records in her diary her cat's last days, emphasizing their gentle bonds for posterity.

On the morning of 2 September, Ba Dinh Square is bathed in golden autumn light. The mood is *fantastic*. Viet Minh students in white shirts blow whistles and 'orchestra leaders' lead cheering sections. The streets are bedecked in red bunting, red banners, and red, fluttering flags. Hanoi's factories and shops are closed. Market places are deserted. Young and old packing the streets have no idea what is going on except that somebody is going to make a big speech. Even Buddhist monks and Catholic priests, not to mention inveterate alcoholics of the Metropole Hotel bar, join the pulsing throng.

An honor guard surrounds a hastily assembled speakers' platform. A thin old man with a broad forehead, bright eyes, and a sparse beard appears. He wears an old hat, a high-collared khaki tunic, and white rubber sandals. A voice at the microphone introduces him as the liberator of the nation.

A rhythmic *'doc lap, doc lap'* rises in the air, 'independence, independence'. Enjoying the cheer and echo, he raises his hand as a sign to be silent. His speech is made of calm, precise words. 'All men are created equal,' he begins. One can hear faint traces of a Nghe An Province accent. President Ho Chi Minh continues, 'The creator has given us certain inviolable rights: the right of life, the right to be free, and the right to achieve happiness.'

This is music to the ears of American OSS operatives who stand by the platform, especially Major Archimedes L.A. Patti, who consciously adapted Ho's paraphrasing of the American Declaration of Independence. The French Commissioner and his officials, by contrast, are ashen-faced. There will be hell to pay. This sounds like a *fait accompli*. An expeditionary force will have to be sent in to restore order.

'Can you hear what I'm saying?' There is a pause. The crowd roars back in approval, 'YES!' 'These immortal words are taken from the Declaration of Independence of the United States of America in 1776. In a larger sense, this means that all people on earth are born equal; all the people have the right

to live, to be happy to be free. Those are undeniable truths.'
A band strikes up 'The Star-Spangled Banner'. OSS operatives
applaud vigorously.

Ho Chi Minh has wandered alone through various regions
of the globe for some thirty-five years, hoping that he would
one day return to Hanoi. Ho can best be described as one of
the luckiest Comintern operatives of all time. He was out
of reach in a Hong Kong jail when Stalin ordered the Great
Purge of nearly all Comintern agents.

For a long time in the spring of 1945, Ho lay low in the
background. There were rumors that he went from house
to house while the Viet Minh infiltrated Hanoi. He was a
strange-looking figure, a cross between a *'can bo'* straight out
of the paddy fields, and a scholar from Saigon. He came clad
in shorts and a brown colonial helmet, carrying a walking
stick. A packet of American cigarettes sticking out of his shirt
pocket summed up his power.

Then the order came down to go from 'pre-revolution' to
'general revolution'. Compact groups of students in white
materialized in the streets, distributing streamers and leaflets
and chanting slogans in rhythm. The gatherings grew more
mixed, with a higher proportion of coolies and women,
the latter dressed in yellow turbans and bright green sashes.
Fluttering red flags and bunting gave the final order. 'Support
President Ho Chi Minh', 'Independence or Death', said
the banners.

In the spring, operatives of the OSS worked with Ho in the
Tonkin jungle. The American officers filed glowing reports on
Ho and even used graphology methods to sketch his psychological make-up. They pointed to the fact that he had helped
American airmen who had been downed in the remote mountains and treated them with utmost respect. He even asked to
meet with an American general and requested a signed picture
of him.

The reports praise his desire to clarify everything. He can be lunatic and stubborn. Ho fixedly resists Japanese imperialism and fights feudalism. Neat, methodical, modest, open, and full of enthusiasm, energy, and initiative. Conscientious.

— ◆ —

On a cloudy Sunday morning, a Japanese delegation comes aboard the crowded deck of USS *Missouri*, anchored in Tokyo Bay. Thousands of seamen are watching while cameramen record every gesture from every conceivable part of the superstructure.

Emperor Hirohito is not coming today. Other royal blood relatives in the government made their excuses. General Yoshijirō Umezu threatened to commit *seppuku* rather than attend, but the emperor prevailed upon him to take part in the ceremony. In their morning dress and top hats and uniforms, the Japanese stand in the public gaze and feel like penitent boys waiting for the school master. The deck is packed to suffocation.

The emperor's representatives all stand at attention as a prayer is said in a language they don't understand. 'The Star-Spangled Banner' plays on a tinny, scratched record. Then, at 9.02 a.m., General Douglas MacArthur approaches the microphones. He moves with an odd air of studied informality. On the threshold of old age, this new shogun looks almost athletic.

As he finishes his brief peroration, the sun suddenly breaks through the clouds. A steady drone above turns into a deafening roar. They planned this well. Some 400 B-29 Superfortresses and 1,500 fighters zoom overhead. At 9.23 a.m. on 2 September 1945, the war is officially over.

As supreme commander of the Allied Powers, MacArthur refused the Soviet demand to occupy the northernmost of

The surrender, 2 September 1945: spectators and photographers pick vantage spots on the deck of USS *Missouri* in Tokyo Bay to witness the formal Japanese surrender proceedings. (NARA NAID: 148727264 Local ID: 111-SC-210644)

The Japanese representatives come aboard *Missouri*. (Australian War Memorial AWM 040960)

As Supreme Allied Commander, General Douglas MacArthur signs the surrender document during the formal surrender ceremonies on USS *Missouri*. (NARA NAID: 520694 Local ID: 80-G-348366)

Japan's four main islands, Hokkaido. He looks forward to the demilitarization and economic rebuilding of Japan. This involves creating a liberal constitution that gives women the right to vote and eliminates ultra-nationalism; imposing land reform; and facilitating the rise of a free press.

— ✦ —

A lavish reception for Lord Mountbatten is held at Rangoon's exclusive Orient Club. Aung San, the fearless local resistance leader, presents him with a Japanese officer's dagger. Aung San's deep bass voice contrasts with his boyish looks. He displays his irrepressible sense of humor with a stream of cynical wisecracks. Mountbatten likes pranks and treats him affectionately. He can see at once that his troops adore him, and when civil government is restored in Burma, Aung San's provisional government should be asked to join.

A man from the highest echelons of the British Empire, Mountbatten is a stickler for protocol. While the elder Burman statesmen, in their pink and mauve headdresses, sit at the top table, Aung San has been placed far away at a lower table. His name is not even included on the toast list. Mountbatten insists that Aung San be called on to make a toast; otherwise, he will not speak. Under his wife Edwina's influence, he has pushed hard in London to include advocates for Burmese independence in the post-war negotiations.

Addressing the audience in fluent English, Aung Sang begins by paying compliments to Mountbatten. Then the speech builds into an almost comic syllogism: 'The principles of an Act may be all right when the Act is passed [pause], but the principles are liable to be undermined by the rules framed under the Act [pause] and the rules again undermined by directives [pause] and the directives by the whims and fancies of the persons executing them.'

Mountbatten enjoys this outspoken view of the reality of British imperialism. As he listens to Aung San, he makes a mental note to tell him that he should decide to be either a Wellington or a Churchill. You cannot be a soldier and a political leader at the same time.

— ✦ —

After Emperor Hirohito's surrender as many as 200,000 Allied soldiers are said to be starving in appalling conditions. 'I want you to go to those boys, wherever they are, and help them to get out as soon as you can,' Mountbatten urges his wife, Edwina. 'I want you to use your own initiative, but you can appeal to any of my military commanders for help. I can accept nothing less than an all-out effort.' Edwina rises to the challenge.

At Nakom Nayok, Lady Mountbatten finds her cousin, Harold Cassel, who has been missing for three and a half years.

Close-up of Lady Mountbatten, wearing the uniform of the St John Ambulance Brigade, sitting in the drawing room of her house in Belgrave Square, London. (Imperial War Museums Collections, TR 1553)

In that time, Harold's hair has turned snow white. Days later, he writes her a thank-you note:

Dear Cousin Edwina,
I felt I must write and tell you how thrilled and grateful all the prisoners here were and are for your visit.

You will realize what a tremendous moment it was for everyone to see a white woman, a real English woman, after so many years. The men particularly admired you coming right into a danger zone – there's an armed Japanese division two miles away. As far as discipline goes, your visit was worth two companies of M.P.s.

Personally, I was thrilled to see you again and most grateful for the family news you brought. It was a kind thought to ring up Ione and get the latest, and I shall never forget it.

Goodbye. With lots of love, from Harold.

— ✦ —

Dan Kiley couldn't believe his luck when he was flying with the top brass from London to Frankfurt. Kiley is so excited about his 'Jackson International Military Tribunal Project' that he runs past generals on the staircase. He is gently reminded to walk behind or to the right. In a few months, his face will appear in Pathé newsreels. Sitting in a movie house in New Hampshire, his wife will shriek, 'That's him!'

The old city of Nuremberg is in ruins, except for the church and the courthouse. The survivors inhabit the cellars and basements of bombed-out buildings. The courthouse complex covers nearly six blocks.

At the presentation, Kiley explains to the generals that the building has been bombed in five places. Repairs are needed to house the prison inmates in the back. The work crews will have to break into the basement to put in trunk telephones and electricity. He shows a blueprint of the dock for the defendants, the prosecution, the judges, the press room, and the interpreters' box – 650 offices are planned.

Usually, this sort of project takes two years to complete; Kiley has just over two months. He is given a staff car, a driver, and two letters of recommendation to track down available construction materials. He is trying to create a unified, orderly, and dignified courtroom, even designing tables in birch and black walnut. Five hundred soldiers are put to work: 250 former Wehrmacht soldiers and 250 former SS soldiers. Brick and stone are passed from hand to hand across the buildings. They have to open a glass factory to create the interpreters' booths.

One day, Kiley walks into a movie house in another town and requisitions rows of seats, all red plush. Whenever a general turns his request down, Kiley just shows him his letters from President Truman and General Eisenhower.

Kiley finds a type of blond plywood with a modern feel for the International Military Tribunal. For a moment, Kiley thinks that the benches for the Nazi VIPs don't deserve backs, but he changes his mind. They can't sit all day without a back, right?

— ◆ —

Two young mothers hand two babies to the proud fathers. A light-headed moment. Both babies were born in a suburb of Johannesburg.

Walter Sisulu's son, Max Vuyisile, was born at home on 23 August and Nelson Mandela's son, Thembi, was born on 23 February. The two fathers stand proudly in front of 7372 Orlando Street near Johannesburg. They can hear the gentle banter coming from inside the house, 'Are you going to be all right?' The house has cement floors, a ceiling, and a tap in the backyard. Both fathers stand in the street, hesitant to share their true feelings about that meeting in the house of Dr Alfred Xuma.

Carrying their babies kindles in them a desire to give a meaningful life to that new generation. The two young fathers lack political experience but share tribal roots, common jokes, and agonizing fears. They want to control their own future, to assert their African identity, not letting the white leadership dictate the terms of the struggle.

They obsessively return to the question of close contacts with Indian delegates. The leadership should be African. Later, they will each say, 'We were never young. There were no dances, hardly a cinema, but meetings, discussions, every night, every weekend.'

Indeed, the Sisulu home functions as the overcrowded quarters of young political activists. Ma Sisulu cooks many meals to accommodate sudden arrivals. Spirited political discussions are regularly interrupted by the roar of trains between Phefeni and Phomolong stations. In that small, overcrowded house, together with Lembede, Mda, Tambo, and Nkomo, they drafted a constitution-manifesto and mustered enough courage to visit Xuma. The head of the ANC lived at his rather grand house in Sophiatown.

As a distinguished doctor, Xuma had studied in the United States, Britain and Hungary. He had completely reorganized the chaotic finances of the ANC. He had played a key role in the drafting of the 'African Claims' document, which demanded full citizenship rights for all Africans. He had linked that demand to the Atlantic Charter drawn up by Churchill and Roosevelt in 1941. Yes, he favored self-determination.

In his aloof, authoritarian way, Dr Xuma carried himself with an air of superciliousness. In a paternalistic way, he had told the young delegation that their committee should start off by not antagonizing anyone, that the Africans as a group were too disorganized and too undisciplined to participate in a mass campaign barefooted, as it were. Dr Xuma was not just skeptical: he was sarcastic.

By the end of the tense meeting, Dr Xuma had reluctantly agreed to the creation of the Youth League, provided the fees would be channeled into the ANC. Strangely, it was Xuma who had created this group, which he called 'the graduates'. He planned to cultivate a new leadership of distinguished young men.

By now, Sisulu has completely forgotten the prophetic warnings he issued in a speech to his wife Albertina, then a very young nurse, at their wedding in 1941: 'Let me warn you, you are marrying a man who is already married. He is married to the nation.'

— ◆ —

In Paris, theater spectators flock to the world premiere of Albert Camus' play, *Caligula*. A young, sensitive actor by the name of Gérard Philipe has the lead role.

The end of the play is disconcerting. When Caligula is assassinated, the mirror he gazes at explodes. As co-conspirators stab him in the back and face, Caligula laughs and screams at the top of his lungs, 'I AM STILL ALIVE!'

As spectators leave the theater and head for Saint-Germain-des-Prés cafés, they are naturally expected to debate the *existential* insinuations of his last words. Most spectators completely miss the message of the play. They see in Caligula an antique version of a Führer.

Camus is shocked but not in the least bitter. In his eyes, there is not one tyrant, but as many Caligulas as there are human minds. Everyone carries a parcel of evil. It is all too easy to lay all the blame at the feet of one tyrant.

— ✦ —

One is almost tempted to withhold her name, for she is a universal archetype, just short of 50 and in love with her kitten. Dawn Powell lives in Greenwich Village. It doesn't matter that during the war she published a commercially successful novel or that she will be rediscovered posthumously. On 29 September, she endures unbearable moments witnessing her cat waste away. She records their last intimate moments together in her diary: 'My dear cat Perkins died today – very sweetly, very quietly, daintily, a lady wanting to give us as little trouble as possible.'

Dawn Powell went out of her way, not so much to save her but to alleviate her pain, cashing a bad check to take her to the vet. She tried to give pills and medicine, which she rejected. Later, she heard her choke. In their last moments together, they locked eyes, her cat managing to fix her eyes on her while Dawn held her paw and moistened her lips with water.

October

In Paris, Christian Dior congratulates Pierre Balmain on his spectacular fashion debut.

In Buenos Aires, smelly, 'shirtless' workers demonstrate in the center of town to bring back to power Juan and Eva Perón. They pee in the fountains.

In Manchuria, Soviet troops are plundering to the dismay of Chang Kai-shek's emissary.

A weary young British officer with plenty of combat experience meets an elderly American civil servant with no combat experience whatsoever. They share a table in the Marble Room of the Nuremberg Grand Hotel.

At a *bal masqué* in Weston, Connecticut, Peggy Guggenheim jitterbugs in a Venetian dress until five in the morning, without any underwear. Nothing to be surprised about. In the Philippines, General Yamashita puts up a spirited defense at his war crimes trial.

Pierre Balmain has just made his triumphant debut. Discreet in color, his dresses espouse the movement of the wearer. His new line is geared to modern living. Christian Dior watches his friend's success with interest. The two worked together during the war.

Dior is a plump, pink-cheeked, balding bachelor of 51. He is fond of sketching *petites gravures* in the silence of his bathtub. He also likes to take long walks by himself on the beach at Granville. He hates the return of smelly petrol cars to Paris. A true gentleman, Dior hesitantly toys with the idea of opening a fashion house, where clothes would give an impression of simplicity while hiding elaborate workmanship. The work would be aimed at a clientele of elegant women.

So, what is stopping Dior? Dealing with sinister businessmen.

— ◆ —

'Everybody is demanding my head, but thus far no one has come to get it,' Juan Perón tells Eva Duarte, while munching a chorizo sandwich.

The two lovers have lived in Calle Posadas opposite one another on the same landing. He was 48 and she was 24 when they first met. He convened with his army cronies in her kitchen. In Argentina, a man never lives with or marries his mistress, but this mighty general depends on her sage advice every day and every night.

The military, hated her, demanding she retire to a private life. She led him by the nose. She dared to rest her arm on the back of the presidential chair on the day of a minister's nomination – the serpent! Polite society cried foul. Her arms were too white, too bare, too bejeweled. He was the vice president, and she pulled the strings.

'The president feels that you should resign,' his closest collaborators had told Perón in an effort to force his hand. They were supposed to be his friends. He wrote and signed his resignation letter, 'I've written it in my own hand, so all can see that my hand has not trembled'.

News traveled fast. At the Belgrano radio station, where Eva worked, the owner told her, 'Your boyfriend has been sacked', drawing a finger across his throat. 'You're out too.' Having previously given her a gigantic raise, he now canceled all her broadcasts. Blackguard. She was the youngest of five illegitimate children, an actress and a familiar voice: the voice of the people on the radio. '*Amigas!* Friends!'

At home, she told him to pull himself together and act like a man. Eva worked the phone and invited junior officers to come to their place, urging them to show heroism, to reveal their patriotism. She called Colonel Velazco, the police chief at the Federal Police Headquarters who had been fired minutes after Perón, to suggest that gloating newspapers be shut down.

In the evening, Perón invented a pretext to return to the Ministry of Labor. Not by coincidence, microphones appeared before him. Bareheaded and in civilian uniform, Perón announced that he had signed two decrees before he left: a salary raise and a new fluctuating, vital minimum wage, – plus a share of the profits. He asked the workers to remain calm: 'I ask you to respect public order so that we may follow our triumphant march; but one day, if it becomes necessary, I will ask you to fight.' The speech was carried live as Eva had planned it. He added that he was a simple citizen now.

'No, no, no! We want you back!' the crowds roared.

At Campo de Mayo, officers listened to the speech carried over state radio. They looked at the resignation document in their hands. Who does he think he is? Newspaper offices were raided. That same night, on 11 October, Juan and Eva slipped out of town to a resort at the mouth of the delta of the River Plate. There, for a day, they enjoyed warm spring sunshine amid the high reeds, listening to the chaos on the radio.

Finally, at one in the morning, as they were asleep in their cottage, the new police chief and young naval cadets came under orders to arrest them, escort them to a gun boat, and drop them on the prison island of Martín García. She cursed them, screamed obscenities, and spat in their faces.

Some say Eva subsequently did nothing, that she spent nights crying over the shoulder of a fellow actress. Others say she flung herself into the streets, descending into the poor quarters, where workers toiled for fourteen hours a day to meet labor leaders. Nearly all workers had missed out on the grain and meat boom to feed starving Europe. The peso's exchange rates had risen to dizzying heights and, here in Argentina, the workers were starving.

Look at the boom-town atmosphere of central Buenos Aires. Fifty-six roulette tables and the wheels spinning all day in the summer resort town of Mar del Plata. And the ordinary working people cannot make ends meet?

Eva lavished funds on labor leaders in charge of the meat-packers. They were the toughest and most disorderly of workers, lowly *descamisados*, 'shirtless ones'. Vociferous row-dies, they were. From the cobbled, odorous dockside avenues, which drain peculiarly foul carcasses, they came, brought in by trucks from the southern districts. A muddy stream, a browned-skinned populace who had never dared to enter the center of town, never ever reached Plaza de Mayo. They streamed over the bridges of the Riachuelo.

Store owners pulled down their metal shutters. The air smelled of perspiration, dirt, and alcohol. The 'shirtless' meatpackers embraced, clasping each other around the strong shoulders, gathering under the balconies of the Casa Rosada. The name Evita – Little Eva – had not been roared yet but soon would. The people screamed obscenities, laughed too loudly, and washed their hands and feet in the fountains of the historic square.

— ✦ —

On 17 October at one o'clock, the Chinese delegation in Changchun meets with the highly decorated Marshal Rodion Yakovlevich Malinovsky's team at the Soviet headquarters. The meeting lasts about three hours. Both sides speak through an interpreter, which slows down the tempo of negotiations considerably.

This is their second meeting to discuss, among other things, Soviet procedures for evacuating their troops. Shortly after the Germans surrendered, the Soviets invaded Manchuria, and they are not eager to leave.

Malinovsky is a highly decorated Soviet commander who fought at Stalingrad and captured Vienna. Under his command, the Red Army crushed the 700,000-strong Japanese Kwantung Army in ten days. Malinovsky is fantastically difficult to pin down. At times, he has his own suggestions and timetables, at other times, he says he must defer to Moscow. Back and forth.

The Chinese write everything down. Indeed, Chang Kia-ngau files regular reports to the personal attention of Chiang Kai-shek while also keeping a diary. Chang Kia-ngau is a high civil servant, an exemplary Mandarin. He can best be described as a Confucian scholar who received a Western education in Japan, studying economics and currency reform.

Every now and then, Malinovsky reiterates his intentions for evacuating his troops northwards between 15 and 20 November, and on 30 December, at the latest, his troops will withdraw into the Soviet Union, after which Chinese troops can take over the defense. Chinese troops are not to land until the Soviets leave.

Would a small contingent of Chinese military be allowed beforehand?

Yes, when Soviet troops withdraw.

Malinovsky's answers and explanations are muddled. Generally speaking, the Soviets do not object to the Chinese taking over administrative powers in the north-east, with the exception of all factories operated during the war by the Japanese, which the Soviets consider to be war booty – quite an exception. An impassive Chang Kia-ngau nods thoughtfully. The day before, Chang learned from various envoys who flew in that 'they' are confiscating all raw materials. 'They' are dismantling and removing the generators in the power plants, as well as communication equipment, and office furniture. Meanwhile, north of Harbin, they are also changing the standard gauge of 4ft 8.5in to a wide Soviet norm of 5ft.

— ◆ —

'Sit down, Major,' insists a man with an American drawl. That voice belongs to a small, careworn, ill-fitting uniform; it belongs to the chief clerk to the United States Supreme Court. Harold B. Willey is now General Secretary of the tribunal. 'By Gawd ...' is how he begins most of his sentences.

No combat experience. The young British officer and the elderly American civil servant sit at a table in the Marble Room of the Grand Hotel in Nuremberg. They listen to the voice of a German maiden singing a folk song. The same weary song to the same audience every night. The American orders Spanish brandy.

Airey Neave explains that he is a member of the English bar with a university degree in jurisprudence. His task at Nuremberg is to prepare the case against the German criminal organizations and act as liaison with the German attorneys on the list. 'They want November Twenny, though Gawd knows ...' The American tries to be reassuring.

'What am I supposed to do tomorrow afternoon?' Neave asks.

'Why, Major, just shove the bundles into the cells.'

The Nuremberg Trial must live up to the highest principles of fairness, but maybe this is something premature. With his cherubic features, the officer looks extraordinarily young.

'Well, Major, I guess it's time for bed. See you in my office in the morning.'

On the morning of Friday, 19 October 1945, Neave dresses in his best service dress. His Sam Browne is gleaming. It feels like he has been ordered to attack at dawn. Neave has never addressed generals or ministers. In the American's office, the two work out a formula to be repeated to every defendant.

Willey knows the stakes. Each defendant is entitled to a fair trial. He summons an American–German lieutenant as interpreter. Then he orders two soldiers to carry copies of the indictments.

The prison's commandant is US Army Colonel Burton Andrus. His voice is high-pitched but authoritative. He is dressed in a green uniform tunic and his burnished, dark-green helmet catches your attention, as does the riding crop tucked under his arm. A hard-assed, by-the-book, rules and regulations bulldog, and a joke among courtroom lawyers.

A sharp cry of command as the master-sergeant salutes the visitors. A high window at the far end of the prison and a spiral staircase to the upper rows of cells against the bright autumn sun. A guard placed at each cell window.

'I am Major Neave, the officer appointed by the International Military Tribunal to serve you with a copy of the indictment in which you are named a defendant.' He faithfully repeats the opening formula while Andrus and Willey stand by. Neave is surprised by his own self-assurance.

Dr Kelley, the psychiatrist, is taking notes. Further behind, Henry Gerecke, the Lutheran prison chaplain, tries to read the emotions of the Nazi defendants. The crowded, pent-up rage of the white helmets by the door is truly astonishing.

'I am also asked to explain to you Article 16 of the Charter of the Tribunal.' A copy is handed to the defendant. 'If you will look at paragraph (c). You have the right to conduct your own defense before the tribunal or to have the assistance of counsel.'

The clang of doors. Odd, menacing silence and then the master-sergeant's bunch of keys. The space between the platform thickly covered in wire netting.

What will he remember of this October afternoon? Willey, a fine man, a true procedural genius. Neave's thoughts drift to Colonel Andrus, dressed in his green, four-pocket uniform tunic. Neave had been struck by the brass buttons imprinted with the United States coat of arms: an eagle carrying thirteen arrows in one talon and an olive branch in the other.

Neave had lived. He had lived. It occurred to him once more how lucky he had been to survive this bloody war. As they walked down to serve the indictment to Göring, his thoughts were besieged by the memory of the 500 ordinary men and women from France, Belgium, and Holland who were executed by the Nazis for helping airmen escape. What sort of trial, if any, had they been allowed?

Göring's cruel and greedy eyes. Neave could remember sheltering from the cold and the Leipzig Police in a cinema in 1942 after escaping from Colditz Castle, hoping to catch a train to the south and to freedom. Göring appeared on the screen. 'So, it has come,' Göring repeated.

After Göring, everything turned into a blur in Neave's mind. Time to repair to the Grand Hotel to hear that same song again.

Göring had the bearings of a leader, but Ribbentrop, Hess, and Streicher left an impression of fanatical mediocrity. All the same. Streicher exposing himself like a monkey in a cage. Frank, Funk, and Frick: The Three F's.

The two alcoholics: Kaltenbrunner and Ley. Kaltenbrunner's tears of self-pity. The slave merchants: Sauckel and

Speer. The more civilized members of Hitler's entourage: Baron Constantin von Neurath and Franz von Papen. An imperial balls-up. The self-confident, frosty, and irritable Schacht. 'You can't hang a banker,' said the cynics in the Marble Room. Jodl – the German admiral had immediately asked for a specialist of the law of the sea to buttress his *to quoque* arguments.

He, Airey Neave, is standing inches from Field Marshal Keitel, dressed in his field marshal's tunic, without badges and decorations and in carpet slippers. His trembling mouth. His limp and unmilitary moustache. Carpet slippers!

It was Keitel who had carried out the orders of Hitler by which six of his Royal Marine Commandos were executed at Bordeaux in December 1942. They were in uniform. His thoughts drift to these men, his Cockleshell Heroes in green berets. He imagines their terror as they stand at attention before the firing squads. After 1941, this man had seldom respected the Geneva Convention. Keitel must pay.

— ◆ —

It's the fifth birthday of the American art magazine *View!* All surrealists are likely to show up. In her barn in Weston, Connecticut, Alice de Lemar gives an enormous *bal masqué*. She has a barn completely renovated for the lavish but simple costume ball, installing a kitchen, bathrooms, and a hardwood floor. The painter Pavel Tchelitchew is in charge of decorations, arranging huge stalks of corn and wheat, and paper streamers to intimate a rustic ballet setting.

The party begins at 10 p.m. The dance band is perfect. A huge bonfire can be seen at a distance to guide the guests. Another field is cleared to park the cars. Two hundred guests are invited but many more show up. The costumes are bizarre, beautiful, hilarious. Two boys dressed in nuns' habits arrive on roller skates. A procession of ten young men and women in single file arrives, all dressed in red as Santa Claus. A British judge impersonator adjusts his wig, while another tips his laurel wreath.

At about three in the morning, supper is served. Peggy Guggenheim whirls by in a Venetian gown, a tricorn upon her head. She jitterbugs until five in the morning. The hoops of her dress billow up to reveal that she has absolutely nothing on underneath that dress.

— ✦ —

General Yamashita had surrendered to American forces in early September, and MacArthur had picked up the case with alacrity. This trial will serve its political purpose admirably. The locals will be grateful, because they suffered terrible losses, and the American public will be grateful because many of its boldest lost their lives in the Philippines. 'The Tiger of Malay' is the ideal scapegoat. In his endeavor to protect Hirohito in Tokyo, General MacArthur wastes no time.

At this stage, humans cannot grasp that MacArthur will meet his match, but what will happen in the Philippines is, to a certain extent, MacArthur's turf. Japanese troops had embarrassed him there. Yamashita had held out on Corregidor with a small fraction of MacArthur's troops. His starving troops and pitifully ill-equipped forces had survived in the Luzon Mountains for eight months. He only surrendered after Emperor Hirohito intervened.

Yamashita is charged as a war criminal on 25 September and arraigned on 8 October. At the arraignment, the defense counsel points out that nowhere in the bills of particulars is it alleged that the accused ordered, condoned, or even knew anything about a list of sixty-four sets of crimes committed by Japanese troops in the Philippines.

General Tomoyuki Yamashita enters Manila courtroom. (Sig Meyers, US Army Signal Corps, Harry S. Truman Library & Museum, NAID: 348544414 Local ID: 2013-2313)

A five-man military commission – three major generals and two brigadier generals – hears the case. No one among the five judges is a lawyer by training. That's not all. On 27 October, close to sixty further violations are introduced to the dismay of the seven-person defense team. On 29 October, Yamashita is put on trial as a war criminal for his life. No time for preparation. A procedure unworthy of our traditions and the immense sacrifices we have made to advance our ideals. Needless and unseemly haste, Your Honor.

The diaries of Japanese soldiers are particularly damning. Machine-gunning, burning, bayoneting, cheerful singing. War-crazed and drunken soldiers. For a month, the world's leading newspapers relay dreadful news of women weeping uncontrollably, babies in the air, and bayonets. Raped nuns are paraded in court, young girls lift their skirts to show the scars. Extensive coverage day after day. Book of Horror.

He needs the best translator to clear up the misunderstanding. Yamashita is an eloquent, impressive speaker. He clings tenaciously to the story that he suffered poor communications and a system of divided command. Victor's Justice. He smiles with half-closed eyes under the bright Klieg lights in the courtroom.

'I believe that under the foregoing conditions, I did the best possible job I could have done. I absolutely did not order any atrocities, nor did I ever permit such a thing, and I will swear to heaven and earth concerning these points. To heaven and earth.'

General Yamashita's defense counsel (L to R): Colonel H.F. Clarke, Captain M. Sandberg, and Captain A.F. Reel. (NARA NAID: 348544604 Local ID: 2013-2315)

General Yamashita after hearing the verdict of his trial. (NARA NAID: 348545078 Local ID: 2013-2316)

November

At a press conference in Berlin, a young intelligence officer by the name of Hugh-Trevor Roper confirms that Hitler is dead. Anna Akhmatova welcomes a gifted conversationalist from Oxford in her tiny Leningrad flat. Georgia O'Keefe sees a derelict house in Abiquiu, New Mexico, and asks a friend whether she should buy it.

All Nazi bigwigs plead not guilty at the Nuremberg Trial. In his opening statement, Justice Jackson explains the stakes of this trial for crimes against peace: 'The wrongs which we seek to condemn and punish have been so calculated, so malignant, and so devastating that civilization cannot tolerate their being ignored, because it cannot survive their being repeated.'

Anna Freud receives a letter from Vienna that passed censorship and was brought by an American. Despite the good news in the letter, she promptly falls ill for five weeks. Is this a coincidence or is her ego or superego letting her down?

Finland's estimated 80,000 children that were sent to Sweden during the war for safekeeping are sent back home. A great many Swedish parents are devastated.

On 1 November, the British are holding a press conference at the Adlon Hotel in Berlin. A senior British intelligence officer tells the assembled correspondents that they can abandon their feverish search for Hitler in the gothic grottos of the Alps and lonely Bavarian latifundia, castle-crowned rocks and mist-enshrouded islands in the Baltic seas. He is dead – dead, burnt, and dissipated on 30 April 1945.

Hugh Trevor-Roper has interviewed seven witnesses, including a guard detective, Bormann's secretary, and Hitler's chauffeur. He treats the evidence with skepticism, admitting that the only proof that Hitler is dead would be the discovery and identification of the body.

A mass of first-hand evidence has been collected and sifted. Hugh Trevor-Roper recounts what he calls the 'dark period' between 22 April, when the Nazi elite left Berlin, and 2 May, when the Russians reached Hitler's bunker. On the last day of his life, after a strange wedding breakfast, Hitler had his Alsatian dog killed, and some hours later said goodbye to about twenty people, half of them women, whom he had summoned from other bunkers. Twelve hours later, a transport officer was ordered to collect about 200 liters of petrol. He managed to gather between 160 and 180 liters, which he placed in the garden just outside the emergency exit of the bunker.

There was no witness to the suicide, but apparently Hitler shot himself through the mouth – the bloodstained sofa was later found in the bunker – and Eva Braun took poison. The bodies were taken into the garden and placed side by side about 3 yards from the emergency exit. Goebbels, Bormann, and perhaps two other witnesses were present. One threw a petrol-soaked rag onto the bodies. Those present stood at attention, gave the Nazi salute, and quickly withdrew back inside the bunker because of the shelling. If and how often the bodies were re-soaked with petrol, and how long they burned, is not known. Nevertheless, the evidence of Hitler's death is positive, circumstantial, consistent, and independent.

— ✦ —

There is a rumor that Leningrad bookstores carry a rich array of pre-revolutionary artifacts, no doubt because so many of their owners died of malnutrition during the 900-day siege. They tried to barter their precious tomes for a crumb of bread. Scores of heavy volumes were stacked by the doors of bookstores in a vain attempt to save them.

On 12 November, a temporary First Secretary of the British Embassy in Moscow sets off on the *Red Arrow* overnight train. He is accompanied by Brenda Tipps, a representative of the British Council. After supper in the dining car, they return to their sleeper. On the top bunk, Isaiah Berlin reads a profusion of newspapers, then, when it's time to switch lights off, he pushes them unceremoniously to the floor as though they are discarded toys tossed out of his pram. In her diary, Brenda Tipps notes that she is in the company of a young, shy All Souls don who speaks incessantly, a mask for his innate shyness, although his logorrhoea could also merely be an indefatigable desire to please.

Our Oxford specialist of the history of ideas is keen to retrace some steps from the past. As a toddler, he witnessed the February and October Revolutions with his governess, observing crowds of mad protesters ferreting out and executing government agents on the spot. His family had left Petrograd for Riga and then fled to London.

After checking into a scarcely heated Astoria Hotel, with faded remnants of past glory, the British visitors head for Angliiski Prospect, where Berlin's family used to live. The inner courtyard looks dank and derelict. Berlin feels like running his hands over what remains of broken railings by the shop in the basement with its misspelled sign '*Shamovar*'. Nothing to cheer about here. The survivors of Leningrad still look emaciated, walking about in their threadbare and tattered clothes across flurries of snow. Some of the heavy bombardment damage has been patched up, but the famous palaces on the outskirts of the city – Tsarskoye Selo, Peterhof, Orianenburg – are off-limits.

At the top of the Nevsky, the British visitors enter the Writer's Bookshop, which seems also to function as a kind of club behind curtains. The small, thin, gray, balding owner, Gennady Moiseyevich Rachlin, invites them into his inner sanctum. He proudly informs his guests that his bookshop sits on the very site of Smirdin's famous establishment! Really? Yes, this is where Belinsky and the Russian writers of the 1830s and 1840s congregated! Really? The British visitors are slightly confused. Does this really matter?

They see a couple of customers gossiping quietly among themselves while leafing through old volumes. There, slumped in a chair in the backroom, is the literary giant: the famous 1920s humorist Zoshchenko – yellowish, pale, confused. Berlin offers his hand but this isn't enough to start a conversation.

Next, the visitors are introduced to a historian by the name of Vladimir Orlov. He explains that virtually every child born during the three years of siege died. Rachlin chimes in to explain that they were kept alive by special rations issued to intellectuals. Yes, you were classed as a 'second-rate writer'. During the siege, a lot of wallpaper was boiled to be able to dilute the glue to make some sort of soup.

Innocently inquiring about the life of subsisting writers in the city, Berlin is startled to hear that Anna Akhmatova still lives here. Where? She is the most eminent pre-revolutionary poet, a giant in her own right and a martyr in the Russian Republic of Letters. There is none like her. Well, Berlin says, I didn't even know she is still alive.

Why, yes of course, comes the reply. She lives not far from here on the Fontanka in Fontanny Dom. Would you like to meet her?

Berlin grows weak in the knees. Orlov steps away to make a phone call and returns with the news that she would receive him this very afternoon at three o'clock.

Berlin accompanies Brenda Tripp back to the Astoria then returns to the bookshop to be introduced to the seductress, the sorceress. The young prodigy, Berlin is well acquainted with the entire Russian literary canon. He knows that this famous beauty shone brilliantly among the Acmeists – the St Petersburg avant-garde and revolutionary circle that used to meet at the legendary Stray Dog Café. To his dismay, Berlin never read a single line of her poetry, but he loves to meet people.

On a snowy, gray afternoon, Orlov and Berlin set off across the Anichkov Bridge with its spectacular bronze horses, walk along the Fontanka Canal and approach the baroque yellow and white plasterwork, with the Sheremetev family heraldry, once the hallmark of the Fontanny Dom. From the inner courtyard, they ascend a dark staircase to the third floor and stop at apartment No. 44 at the end of the hall. Inside, they walk past five or six rooms to reach Akhmatova's place.

Her room overlooks the courtyard. She looks like a tragic, dignified queen, yet there is not the faintest trace of the heart-breaking or melodramatic about her. Berlin bows, which is the least he can do. It is both a formal, barely noticeable bow, one reminiscent of German manners, and it is also a bow that conveys genuine reverence. The tiny place is bare: no carpets, no window curtains, a small table, three chairs, a sofa, a dresser, a bed. There is also a 1911 sketch of Akhmatova by Modigliani when she was in Paris. She is wearing a white shawl around her shoulders.

In the presence of Orlov, the conversation is some-what stilted: having suffered years of denunciation and

vilification, Akhmatova does not trust anyone. As enthusiasm and nostalgia seem to take hold of the exchanges – *The
Dublin Review*, the Blitz in London, an Akhmatova PhD
student in Bologna – echoing from the courtyard one hears
'Isaiah! Isaiah!'

Someone is calling his name as though they're a rowdy
undergraduate in an Oxford Quadrangle. As Berlin mumbles
apologies and rushes downstairs, Randolph Churchill, the son
of the war supremo, wants his friend to come back to the
Astoria Hotel. Randolph doesn't know any Russian and wants
the caviar he just bought to be placed on ice. Orlov seems to
have taken fright and makes a quick exit.

Having made sure the caviar is safely stored with ice, Isaiah
telephones Akhmatova to apologize. 'I shall wait for you at
nine this evening' is her reply. This time, there is an elderly
lady, an expert in Assyrian antiquities, in attendance. How
appropriate, Berlin wonders, aware that he is in the presence
of a dying Cleopatra. She reveals a genuine interest in English
universities. At midnight she takes her leave.

 By the glowing stove, the two conversationalists draw
closer in the dark room, united in their unshakable belief
in the unity of European culture. The young Oxford don is
dimly aware that from 1925 to 1940 she was not allowed to
publish. Thus, nobody in the West knows anything about her
life. She keeps asking him questions about the West and he
keeps digging into the details of her past life.

Akhmatova is glad to hear that one of her former friends
of the Acmeist circle, Salome Andronikova Halpern, is still
alive. She had been a notorious beauty who had frequented
the Stray Dog Café in Petersburg, where she had composed
futurist music for performance. Thanks to her foreign guest,
she learns that her 'Salomé' had married a Russian lawyer in
New York, where she now sustained a vibrant Russian culture
in exile.

As messenger between two cultures, Berlin over the next few hours seeks to understand why Akhmatova did not leave Russia. Akhmatova is categorical that it was never her wish to choose the road of exile. She would never leave her native Russia, her native language, her people. Her descent into misery had begun in 1921 when her husband, Nikolay Gumilev, had been executed on trumped-up charges. Next, her close friend and poet Mandelstam had been arrested. Standing with other women in long queues to deliver packages to him, one woman with bluish lips standing behind her, speaking, like everyone, in whispers, had asked her whether someone could preserve in words this weight of terror. Mayakovsky and Esenin had taken their own lives.

The poems were too dangerous to be written down, and it was a disservice to friends to even share them. 'And it's not clear to me/Who is beast now, who is man/How long before the execution.'

In March 1938, her son, Lev Gumilyov, had been arrested. For seventeen months she had not known whether he was alive or dead. For a while, she had lived the life of a common-law wife with the art scholar Nikolay Punin, and he too had been deported. During the Great Patriotic War, she had been exiled to Tashkent, living in an airless room with Lydia Chukovskaya and Nadya Mandelstam. For the first time she had been allowed to publish a strongly censored volume of *Selected Poems*. By some sort of miracle, her son had returned in the late summer. This, perhaps, she owed to her readings to wounded soldiers in hospitals and to soldiers at the front. On her way back to Leningrad, she had given a public reading at the Polytechnic Museum which had ended with a dangerous rousing public ovation.

At three in the morning, her son, Lev Gumilyov, made his appearance. He was hungry and went into the small kitchen, returning with some boiled potatoes in a small dish, which they all shared. The mother apologized for the threadbare meagerness of her hospitality.

Lev was phenomenally well read, having preserved in himself standards of Western literature, reading Joyce and Proust in the original. For several hours, they discussed canonical authors of Russian literature. Although they hardly agreed on the legacy of each author, Akhmatova's tone frequently veered from dignified queen or dying Cleopatra to the shrewd and humorous. Yes, Pasternak had had several crushes on him, but then again, it *was* Pasternak.

He could not live without her, he kept saying. She spoke about many other past loves. They had talked of the most intimate things, connecting Oxford and Goethe and Mozart. It was light outside and one could hear the freezing rain over the Fontanka courtyard. Dazed, exalted, in love, Berlin got to his feet, kissed her hand, and took his leave. His eyes caught the time on his watch. It was eleven o'clock in the morning.

— ✦ —

On Monday night, 19 November, Georgia O'Keefe receives a letter from her friend, Maria Chabot, saying she heard on the radio of a wonderful washing machine that does everything for you. Really?

Maria can't make up her mind about the house Georgia saw in Abiquiu either. It's an abandoned adobe house that belongs to the Catholic Archdiocese of Santa Fe. It sits on a 3-acre property overlooking the Chama River. Mary Chabot says she knows good people who are respectful of mud.

— ✦ —

The International Military Tribunal trial in Nuremberg is set to begin. Security becomes very tight. Hermann Göring,

View of rubble in
Nuremberg, Germany,
1945–46, at the time
of the Nuremberg
Trials. (NARA NAID:
348537736 Local ID:
2013-3267)

The largely undamaged Palace of Justice in Nuremberg, the location of the trials.
(NARA NAID: 348537736 Local ID: 2013-3267)

the highest-ranking Nazi on trial, is escorted into the court-room. Kiley is standing just a few yards away. No one knows whether he will co-operate, and his attitude might influence the other bigwigs.

Rumors are flying and Kiley knows a lot about Göring. To the French, Göring is scornful; with the Americans, he is charm itself. He is always cautious and respectful to the British. The Russians terrify him. He winces every time a Red Army officer comes near.

Göring is hypothetically the star witness. No one in the Third Reich received more birthday gifts than him. Industrialists for years on end lined up to offer him carpets, statues, first editions, Renaissance paintings, and huge checks.

The Nazi leaders on trial. Hermann Göring (in the box, front row, left) takes notes, and Rudolf Hess (second from left) watches the proceedings intently. Next to Hess is former Foreign Minister Joachim von Ribbentrop. In the back row are Admirals Karl Dönitz and Erich Raeder. (NAID: 350375646 Local ID: 2004-440)

In the summer of 1940, Göring had promised Hitler that his Luftwaffe would win the Battle of Britain on its own.

Kiley is completely overworked. His mind drifts often to Garmisch-Partenkirchen in Bavaria. The mountain hasn't opened yet. There's going to be a fantastic party up there. Guys from the air force are flying planes over. He is thinking that there will have to be a local band, and the opportunity of slaloming with the former German Olympic team. And the Red Cross girls are coming along.

On the opening day of the trials the defendants appear as a group for the first time. They are nondescript and seemingly harmless; one cannot imagine that they once held sway over an entire continent, terrorizing millions of soldiers and civilians.

In accordance with Article 24(a) of the Charter, the tribunal orders that the indictment be read. Despite requests from the prosecutors and defense counsel that this copious catalog of crimes be summarized, the tribunal insists on a full reading. People catch their breath. Two American, two French, and two junior Russian prosecutors will take turns reading.

Meanwhile, people in the courtroom get acquainted with IBM's translation system, turning the dials every now and then. They can't help staring at Hermann Göring, who gestures and mutters loud comments. He can protest only when the verb finally surfaces at the end of the translation into German. His reactions lag, slightly out of tune as he listens to the crimes in his headset.

On the second day, presiding Judge Lawrence calls upon the defendants to plead 'guilty or not guilty', but German defense attorneys object, saying they were unable to consult with their clients that morning. Lawrence has to grant a recess.

At long last, a guard approaches the defendants' dock with a microphone, setting it before Göring, who is on his feet:

Hermann Göring: 'Before I answer the question of the tribunal whether or not I am guilty ...'

The president: 'I informed the Court that defendants were not entitled to make a statement. You must plead guilty or not guilty.'

Göring: 'I declare myself in the sense of the indictment not guilty.'

The president: 'Rudolf Hess.'

Rudolf Hess: 'No.'

The president: 'That will be entered as a plea of not guilty.' [Laughter.]

The microphone is passed along the two rows of defendants. The expressions of 'not guilty' differ:

'I declare myself in the sense of the indictment, before God and the world and particularly before my people, not guilty.'

'Not guilty. For what I have done or had to do, I have a pure conscience before God before history and my people.'

'I declare myself in no way guilty.'

'Not guilty. I answer the question in the negative.'

Despite unanimous 'not guilty' pleas, all defendants are miraculously co-operating. Defendant Göring again tries to steal the limelight. He stands in the prisoner's dock to try to make an elaborate speech:

The president: 'You are not entitled to address the tribunal except through your counsel at the present time. I will now call upon the Chief Prosecutor for the United States of America.'

Mr Justice Jackson: 'May it please Your Honors: The privilege of opening the first trial in history for crimes against
the peace of the world imposes a grave responsibility.
The wrongs which we seek to condemn and punish have
been so calculated, so malignant, and so devastating, that
civilization cannot tolerate their being ignored, because
it cannot survive their being repeated. That four great
nations, flushed with victory and stung with injury stay
the hand of vengeance and voluntarily submit their captive enemies to the judgment of the law is one of the most
significant tributes that Power has ever paid to Reason.'

The translation system produces a captivating hum. Everyone
is listening very closely. The Americans are tense and wonder

Justice Robert H. Jackson delivers the prosecution's opening statement at the
Nuremberg Trials. (NARA NAID: 350375624 Local ID: 2004-430)

whether they will, for once, earn unqualified praise from the British prosecution team: 'What these men stand for we will patiently and temperately disclose. We will give you undeniable proofs of incredible events. The catalog of crimes will omit nothing that could be conceived by a pathological pride, cruelty, and lust for power.'

During the war, Jackson himself did not believe reports of death camps in Poland. The atrocity tales were greeted at first with general skepticism. He now wants to convince the skeptics. He has worked for six weeks on this speech, and he squarely addresses the question of 'victor's justice':

> Before I discuss particulars of evidence, some general considerations which may affect the credit of this trial in the eyes of the world should be candidly faced. There is a dramatic disparity between the circumstances of the accusers and of the accused that might discredit our work if we should falter, in even minor matters, in being fair and temperate.
>
> Unfortunately, the nature of these crimes is such that both prosecution and judgment must be by victor nations over vanquished foes. The worldwide scope of the aggressions carried out by these men has left but few real neutrals. Either the victors must judge the vanquished or we must leave the defeated to judge themselves ...
>
> We must never forget that the record on which we judge these defendants today is the record on which history will judge us tomorrow. To pass these defendants a poisoned chalice is to put it to our own lips as well. We must summon such detachment and intellectual integrity to our task that this Trial will commend itself to posterity as fulfilling humanity's aspirations to do justice.

In the afternoon, reading from captured reports of the SS Einsatzgruppen and the Stroop Report, Jackson gives the court the startling numbers of the murdered. At the end of his address, Jackson explains that the real complaining party at the bar is civilization. Americans are jubilant. This is a tour de force and only Jackson could have pulled this off.

— ✦ —

Anna Freud is dazed. She just received a letter from August Aichhorn in Vienna. Covered with official stamps from the Allied military censor, the letter made its way to London in the suitcase of an American soldier. She likes Aichhorn. He is the only person who managed to take a photograph of her that she likes. The cherished photograph shows her only from the waist up. She thinks herself dowdy and bottom-heavy.

Aichhorn informs her that during the war he moved south of Vienna and managed to treat several psychiatrists. There is also bad news: his wife became ill the year of the Anschluss and never recovered. His apartment in Vienna was bombed out. One of his two sons was deported to a concentration camp.

He tells her that he is ready to reopen the Vienna Psychoanalytic Society. Not least, the Vienna municipality is more than receptive to the idea. Welcome news, yet the letter tears open a Pandora's box of pent-up feelings. Why, then, did the Viennese authorities show so much disdain for her father between 1908 and 1938? If they had not shown such disparaging hostility towards her father's work and ideas, the Vienna Psychoanalytic Society would have a large teaching staff and perhaps even affiliated psychoanalytic institutes.

Anna Freud never has to interrupt her work for health reasons, but she has been hit by the flu and hopes that after three days she might be up and about. For the next five weeks she is incapacitated by pneumonia.

— ✦ —

By the end of November, some 20,000 women have been recruited for 'comfort stations' in Japan. The licensed prostitution program started three days after the Japanese Government accepted defeat. Spearheaded by the bureau heads of the Home and Welfare Ministries as well as the Metropolitan Police Boards, the aim was 'to preserve the chastity of Japanese women from the foul hands of the occupation forces'. One of the reasons for prompt action is no doubt the shattering number of rapes on conquered Okinawa. Another explanation is the customary efficiency of Japanese public services to meet the needs of the arriving US forces.

In early September, representatives of fifty-seven operators from the vast red-light district of Asakusa are called in. The Hypothec Bank is solicited to set aside three-quarters of the necessary funds, granting 24 million yen for the operation. A new English name is born: the Recreation and Amusement Association.

Nevertheless, besides basic shelter issues in ruined Japan, an obstacle raises its ugly head that no public servant or police patrol can solve. Unlike with Japanese servicemen, brothel owners have no sway over United States Armed Forces. They lack legal authority to enforce the use of condoms. Do they really care about *gaijin* outsiders? It is another month or so before occupation authorities notice rapid infection rates, closing some comfort stations and installing prophylactic aid posts.

— ✦ —

In Sweden, he is called a *Finnpojke*, a 'Finnish boy'. He is one of Finland's estimated 80,000 war children, sent abroad for safekeeping. He arrived in the spring of 1942, aged 4. One afternoon in November, Martti Kalervo Broström comes home from school and his foster parents show him a telegram concerning his single mother, Aili, back home. She has died from kidney disease. Since the spring, Martti had heard about a serious illness and a hospital stay. He had struggled with both sorrow and pity, and a glimmer of hope that he might stay a while longer with Albert and Selma. In her last will, she had stated that he could stay with them should she pass away, and for this he had forever been grateful. The Swedish authorities did not object to war children remaining in place, but the Finnish authorities were adamant: all Finnish children were to come back home.

The first wave of transport children had left for Sweden as early as 15 December 1939, merely a fortnight after the outbreak of war with the Soviet Union. Two hurriedly freighted ships sailed between Turku and Stockholm, then after submarine attacks in January 1940, train travel had become the exclusive escape route.

Martti had slept on boards placed crosswise across seats. The trains traveled during the night with blacked-out windows, putting a lot of pressure on parents and elderly people during the ten-day ordeal. A fifth of the children had felt terror and become ill. Some had become haunted by the idea that they were punished for disobeying a parent or for displeasing a sibling. The oldest children did not believe this, yet they felt guilty for escaping their country of origin while their biological family continued to be exposed to the dangers of war.

Upon arrival in Sweden, frightening medical exams had taken place, with unconsolable children terrorized by injections and clamoring for their mothers. Those diagnosed with an infectious disease were kept in isolation for weeks.

His future foster parents had applied for a daughter, but when he had appeared in the small southern village of Jönköping, there were two boys – an administrative error.

Fortunately, the young boy with the shaved head shared the same birthday, 31 August, with his future adoptive father, and they had chosen him. Driving home, the foster parents in the front had relied on a dictionary for basic commands, which they later wrote down on cards: 'Come eat', 'Go to sleep'. Luckily, an old lady in Jönköping spoke Finnish, and there were two other transport children in his new surroundings.

By the end of the war, Martti barely recalls his mother and has all but forgotten Finnish. When he needed to write a letter, he had to rely on the elderly lady. Martti had never known his father. His mother had always insisted she was not a 'party girl'.

Martti feels confident he will be able to stay. His foster parents are not demonstrative in their everyday gestures of affection, yet they provide safety. And his foster sisters are kind and protective. Out of the blue, a letter arrives from his father. He insists on adoption, adding that he could not conceive with his new wife. But equally surprising, his maternal grandparents enter the fray, denouncing the new father as a fraud and a liar.

December

The war is over, but will there be peace next year? An exhausted humanity comes to terms with the division of the world at the Yalta Potsdam Conferences.

Two Austrian POWs on the run decide that Lhasa in Tibet is their best chance of finding freedom.

'Did you have a good war?' is now a fashionable cocktail query. Frida Kahlo has to think hard before giving her own appraisal.

At the Second All-Union Classical Music Competition in Moscow, the lights go out just as Sviatoslav Richter is about to play. Is this a coincidence or a direct order from the Kremlin?

Despite earlier refusals, President Truman asks Eleanor Roosevelt to go to London as a representative at the United Nations. On Christmas Eve, Norma Jean, the future Marilyn Monroe, is given an ultimatum.

In Los Angeles, Ingrid Bergman drives to Malibu to spend an afternoon with photographer Robert Capa. In Garmisch-Partenkirchen, American skiers and skaters get ready to celebrate the New Year with Germans.

Heinrich Harrer and Peter Aufschnaiter decide to head across the Changtang Plateau, accompanied by a guide and a donkey. They are betting on the fact that an approach to the forbidden city of Lhasa in Tibet from the north-west might go unchallenged. Dressed in rags of sheepskin, the Austrians Harrer and Aufschnaiter look verminous and starving. They escaped with five others from a POW camp in India twenty months earlier. Disguised as an Indian wire-repairing party, with two dressed as officers, they marched out in broad daylight through the main gate, with the guard presenting arms.

Armed with a compass and map, they light dung fires at night to survive the freezing weather. During the day, they hobble along on frozen ground. The pair has by now traversed more than fifty mountain passes and trudged through 1,000 miles of territory at high altitude.

— ✦ —

'Did you have a good war?' is an incongruous question in a country like Mexico, which was never at war with Germany or Japan. But the Second World War led to a rapprochement and an economic boom, that's for sure. Frida Kahlo likes to end her exchanges on a cheerful note. The first thing that comes to her mind are the self-portraits and the reconciliation with Diego Rivera – in the last few years they have become very close – and how much time he spent by her bedside. He always praises her work in the presence of American visitors and philanthropists: 'Frida is the better painter.'

The war had started for her when she was visiting France in 1939 for the opening of an exhibition. The country was in turmoil. The Louvre had bought one of her self-portraits on glass with an aluminum frame. What does she remember about this war? One memory? The hard corsets pressing against her lungs? Would people be able to remember the songs?

Frida recalls her times with the *Los Fridos* group, when she had become an art teacher to working-class students. She had taught them Communist songs. They called her *La Maestra* and they sang together. She didn't just want to teach them painting but how to live life. On Fridays, she took them to the local market, where fruits and vegetables, puppets and chickens were sold. She wanted them to appreciate *la raza* and their native culture. Some had dropped out, but others would come regularly to her Blue House and were part of *Los Fridos*. She was their sister, mother, teacher, feeder. They had painted a *pulqueria* (bar) in Coyoacán – don't forget *pulqueria* art! The irate owner had painted over the work.

The last thing they painted together was a *lavadoria*, used exclusively by poor women washing other people's clothes. The government set aside the building, and Frida and her students did washing, ironing, sewing, then shared a meal after work. The students graduated just this year. The songs they sang!

— ✦ —

The All-Union musical contest in Moscow was canceled during the war and this event celebrates a return to normal life. The competition this year will have three categories: piano, violin, and cello. The jury is composed of twenty-two illustrious names, among them David Oistrakh, Konstantin Igumnov, Vladimir Sofronitsky, Aleksandr Shtrimer, Semyon Kozolupov, Dmitry Tsyganov, Lev Oborin, and Emil Gilels. Dmitri Shostakovich is appointed chairman of the jury.

The upper-age limit has been extended to 32. One of the beneficiaries of this concession is 31-year-old Sviatoslav Richter. Many believe that the rule has been stretched so that he could take part. The other contender is 26-year-old Viktor Merzhanov, who has served at the front. Both are highly considered.

Richter comes in late for one of the rounds. The tension grows in the hall as the jury is kept waiting. When Richter appears, he is in the company of Prokofiev, and he gives an inspired rendering of the composer's eighth sonata. The conductor discovers that the pages of the score have been muddled.

In the second round, Richter will have to surmount a test of nerves. The lights in the hall will go out as Richter is about to play. Richter waits in sepulchral darkness. Is this a direct order from Stalin? People are aghast. They can hardly breathe. Is his performance canceled?

Richter has nerves of steel. After what seems like an interminable time, candles are placed on the piano. He plays Liszt's *Transcendental Studies*, '*Wilde Jagd*'. The candles bounce and bob on the piano. Merzhanov's performance is Rachmaninoff's third concerto. Merzhanov and Lev Oborin will be co-winners in the piano category. Richter will not win any prize, despite his extraordinary performance.

Cellist Slava Rostropovich will be accused of having chosen an 'unknown' modern work. His uncle sits on the jury and is vehemently opposed to him winning the competition, arguing that he will easily win in future years. Give it to someone else. Slava wins.

— ✦ —

Weeks earlier, her response had been negative: 'Oh, no! It would be impossible. How could I be a delegate to help organize the United Nations when I have no background or experience in international meetings?' Days before Christmas, President Harry Truman follows up with an official letter:

December 21, 1945
My dear Mrs. Roosevelt:

I am pleased to inform you that I have appointed you one of the representatives of the United States to the first part session of the General Assembly of the United Nations to be held in London early in January 1946. A complete list of the government's delegation is enclosed herewith.

You, as representative of the United States ... will bear the grave responsibility of demonstrating the whole-hearted support which this government is pledged to give to the United Nations Organization, to that end that the organization can become the means of preserving the international peace and of creating conditions of mutual trust and economic and social well-being among all peoples of the world. I am confident that you will do your best to assist these purposes in the first meeting of the General Assembly.

Sincerely yours,

Harry S. Truman

In spite of having been kept in the dark as vice president, Truman is working hard to tap into his predecessors' well-established talent pool. The next few months promise to be busy for FDR's widow. The Republicans, the legalists, and the isolationists will doubt her experience and attack her weaknesses. The Soviets, the columnists, and the poor-country diplomats will not give her the benefit of the doubt. A small and dedicated team is what she needs. 'I shall do the best I can' is how Eleanor Roosevelt frames her response to the president. Teddy and Franklin are gone, but there is still a Roosevelt in the game.

— ✦ —

She has shoulder-length California-blonde hair. At nearly 19, the model Norma Jean has a good figure. She has left her factory job and no longer lives with her husband's mother. Photographs of her are appearing in *Swank*, *Sir!*, and *Peek*.

Marilyn Monroe in her pre-stardom days. (Wikimedia Commons)

At Christmas, she finds it impossible to be at home. There is a showdown when she returns. Her husband makes an ultimatum, 'You have to choose between a modeling career and maybe the movies or a home life with me.'

— ✦ —

She starts the engine and emerges out of a short and steep driveway surrounded by lush vegetation, which encloses a chiseled redwood house. Behind her classic sunglasses and the silk scarf over her hair, one cannot recognize her. Driving off 1220 Benedict Canyon Drive, the rather unremarkable Oldsmobile makes a right turn instead of a left.

Ingrid Bergman is not required to show up for work on the set for two days. She doesn't drive east in the direction of RKO Pictures, and her husband doesn't know this. She now glides down Sunset Boulevard to the ocean. She is meeting her

lover, Robert Capa, at the beach house of a friend, the writer
Irwin Shaw, at 18 Malibu Road.

At 30, she is at the zenith of her career. Her transcendent
beauty is known to millions. She receives up to 25,000 letters
a week from adoring fans. Ingrid Bergman likes to portray
characters whose lives have been a little abnormal. Her sen-
suousness is hard to pin down, at once innocent, lush, at the
edge of a volcano.

On the road, Bergman's thoughts drift to the exiled
Hungarian community in Hollywood, arresting and original
human beings. She hears the voice of Michael Curtiz, the wise
Hungarian director:

Ingrid, you're so wrong, that's not what they do in America.
America is typecasting. The audience wants it at the box
office. They pay their money to see Gary Cooper being

Office of War
Information photograph
of Ingrid Bergman
at New York City
canteen with US Coast
Guardsman (left) and
Royal Navy sailor (right).
(OWI Photograph,
National Museum of the
US Navy Lot 9432-3,
Wikimedia Commons)

Gary Cooper, not the hunchback of *Notre Dame*. So, you are going to ruin your career by trying to change and do different things. Do the same thing, play the same sort of role all the time and you develop this one attractive side that the audience will love.

How will it end? They expect you to wear lovely gowns and clothes and to look pretty. She recalls how *Casablanca* was not shot sequentially and no one knew where they were headed.

The Oldsmobile reaches the ocean and heads north on the Pacific Coast Highway. The highway luxuriates in the sea air, catching glinting sparkles that play with the waves and the foam. What will be the end of her liaison with Capa?

She will live another 500 years, and people will believe that Americans went to war for the same reasons that Ilse did in *Casablanca*, Capa once told her, and at the time no one knew the direction of the war. 'You rarely played what you looked like or what you were,' he also told her. A sentence full of resonance.

The romance with Capa started one night at the Ritz Hotel in Paris and was very much a dream-come-true sequence of events. Capa, one of the world's best raconteurs, who spoke 'Capanase', as Hemingway described it, and Irwin Shaw, one of America's best-selling novelists, wrote a note together to lure her downstairs. The initial plan was to send her flowers and invite her to dinner, but after consultation they figured out that they could not do both, so they decided to have a vote on the matter and dinner won by a close margin. But if she didn't care for dinner, flowers could be sent, although they were still debating the question. For fear of running out of talk, and before running out of their limited supply of charm, they would call at 6.15 p.m. Signed: Worried.

It is not known who calls – Capa or Shaw – yet she agrees to meet them at the Ritz basement bar. She is wearing a beautiful haute couture gown and a red flower in her hair. Asked why she agreed to join them, she replies that she would rather spend an evening downstairs than staring at a vase of flowers in her bedroom. 'You said you were going to take me out to dinner,' she said. 'I hope you have enough money because I'm very hungry.' She is giggling and knocking back flutes of the best champagne. The two men invite her to Maxim's for dinner.

Born in Budapest to middle-class Jewish parents, who owned a fashionable dressmaking company, Capa has so far photographed three wars. He has never recovered from the loss of his friend Gerda Taro, who in Paris invented the name 'Capa' and typed his captions. He had hoped to marry her. She was crushed to death by a tank in the Spanish Civil War.

During the Second World War, Capa fell in love with 'Pinky' in London. With American troops, he invaded Tunisia and Sicily. However, one of his best friends eventually married her. Capa's pictures are full of intense compassion, and perhaps no photojournalist had a greater influence on other photojournalists in the twentieth century.

Profligate and passionate, Capa and Shaw invite Bergman to a small night club in Montmartre, where they continue to drink. 'If the pictures are not good enough, you're not close enough,' he tells her with a wry smile. He has hundreds of self-deprecating anecdotes, whether 'lost in fog with a convoy over the Atlantic with foghorns that could be heard in Berlin', 'kissed by hundreds of old women in liberated Tunis', or 'dangling from a parachute in a tree during the Italian campaign'.

As German troops relinquished Paris, he was trying to fit thousands of blurred faces in the viewfinder of his camera. He passed by the house where he had lived for six years. His concierge was waving a handkerchief and he was yelling to her from his rolling tank, '*C'est moi! C'est moi!*'

When the money runs out, Bergman pulls out her purse and the dancing continues into the early hours. Capa sees at once that they are not in the presence of a 'Swedish milkmaid'.

At dawn, she and Capa walk along the banks of the Seine and he ends his string of anecdotes with himself in a pair of trunks woken up by irate security officers. He had taken a nose-cone shot of a Flying Fortress for *Illustrated* and the shot landed on the front cover. So, a group of highly irate United States security officers showed up in his bedroom: was he aware that while he had taken a picture of the nose of a lieutenant in the Perspex cone, he had also photographed one of the most closely guarded and vital secrets of the Flying Fortress bomber?

Beg your pardon, 'That little black thing! That's the A-number-one-secret of the American air force?'

The security officer almost choked. He continued, 'That's the Norden bombsight!'

'What?'

All 400,000 copies of *Illustrated* were recalled and destroyed.

The next day, Bergman joins the USO to entertain troops in Germany, then the two are reunited in Berlin in July. Both had, in fact, started their careers in the German capital. No one would recognize incandescent Ilsa, of Rick's fame, busy as they are pushing their prams. Besides, there is no man above the age of 14 on the streets of Berlin.

The two lovers stumble across an informal, thriving black market at Tiergarten, where hard-up Berliners sell household goods in exchange for food. Red Army soldiers seem to be crazy for watches, especially American Mickey Mouse watches.

Berlin is a devastated city, with ugly pockmarks on every building. Capa sees a bathtub in the middle of a street which is also half-broken. You can walk into it. Imagine that: Ingrid

Bergman as a centerfold, all dressed, in a bathtub in Berlin. His film will get lost, but another photographer catches this intimate street scene.

He likes her for her impish humor, her puckish repartee. Bergman is often invited to dine with the military brass, but she goes out with the enlisted men, takes down their names and addresses and calls their families when she gets back home to America. She has just declined an invitation to lunch with Eisenhower, commenting, 'I really have nothing to say to him'.

Capa tries to warn her about Hollywood and being part of the institution. 'Don't go back,' he says. She tells him to come with her, and they go to the West Coast.

Capa is every inch a gentleman and a *bon vivant*, but 'every inch a gentleman' among Hungarian exiles is not the same as 'every inch a gentleman' among Knightsbridge residents. Capa is terrifically generous with his money, partially because he doesn't care in the least about it. Behind his weary smile and his stream of self-mocking anecdotes, there is an odd sadness and *mal de vivre* about him.

In Paris they celebrate VJ Day when Japan surrenders. She had seen newsreels of how all the girls threw themselves at the soldiers and kissed them on VE Day and she says to Capa, 'I'm going to do that; I'm going to throw myself at somebody and kiss him.'

They are sitting in a Jeep in the Champs-Élysées and Capa asks, 'Which one?'

'Him – over there.' She dashes out of the car, throws herself at the soldier, and kisses him on the mouth. He doesn't think twice about it. He kisses her back.

The Oldsmobile has turned right and is headed north toward Malibu. *I suppose that's where I began to fall in love with him*, she thinks. In Paris, he remarks that after the second bottle of champagne he usually can't remember who he is anymore, and they are now on their third bottle when she has forgotten her name and address. 'I am a gambler,' he tells her, after she invites him to Hollywood. At the end of August, after Hiroshima, Capa thinks that the profession of war photographer is finished forever. He must get into movies. He doesn't really know what he wants.

The two lovers will spend some time on the beach, and in the evening, they will have the house to themselves. The war is over. There is no reason to get up in the morning.

You must remember this
A kiss is just a kiss
A sigh is just a sigh
The fundamental things apply
As time goes by.

Endings and
New Beginnings

January

One of **J. Ted Hartman's** last wartime actions was to march German prisoners to the Russians in Austria, with thirty-six tanks guarding 18,000 POWs, making the entire column over 6 miles long. Hartman later regretted handing these soldiers to the Red Army.

His father and brother-in-law met him at the station of Ames in Iowa at three o'clock on the morning of 15 March 1946. He later became an orthopedic surgeon, serving as Dean of the Texas Medical School. Half a century later, he revisited the Ardennes battleground and was flooded by inordinately vivid and precise memories. The adrenaline rush was back.

— ◆ —

The son of a priest, and not doing well in school, **Hans-Ulrich Rudel** joined the Luftwaffe in 1936. During training, his performance was so disappointing that he was punished and almost banned from the Luftwaffe. By 1943, he had flown over 1,000 missions. He had landed behind enemy lines in Russia to save a stranded friend then swam across the icy River Dniester to escape. Later, seriously wounded by anti-aircraft fire near Frankfurt, he returned to combat with an artificial limb after his leg was amputated. Rudel was not only an ace flyer, he was also a true believer, which is why Göring and Hitler wanted him to stop flying to help indoctrinate the Hitler Youth.

Rudel surrendered to the Americans at the end of the war. In 1948, he immigrated to Argentina, where he joined other active Nazis.

— ✦ —

Frida Kahlo bequeathed some 200 paintings to posterity. From the moment she suffered her horrific bus accident in 1925, Kahlo grieved as much from back pain as from empty promises from surgeons. In her art, Kahlo never succumbed to one school of paint, blending indigenous roots, *Mexicanidad*, and Pre-Columbian motifs. She stayed close to Diego Rivera, to whom she had first shown her work in 1929. They had married the same year, divorced in 1939, and remarried the following year.

Days before her death on 13 July 1953, Kahlo left her sickbed to join a demonstration denouncing the ousting of Guatemalan President Jacobo Árbenz Guzmán by the CIA. She disappeared from view for some twenty years, then gained world fame.

— ✦ —

Raoul Wallenberg saved tens of thousands of Jewish lives. To achieve his aims, he created a protective Swedish passport – a *Schutz-Pass* – which unilaterally announced that it granted the holder immunity. He bought and rented about thirty buildings in Budapest, mostly to cater for children whose parents had been killed or deported. He confronted Nazi officials directly, and often stood on the platforms of trains for last-minute rescues.

After his arrest by Soviet authorities, he disappeared into the Gulag. In 1963, Yad Vashem, the Holocaust Remembrance Center, recognized the bold diplomat as Righteous Among the Nations. The United States Holocaust Memorial Museum is located at 100 Raoul Wallenberg Place SW in Washington DC.

— ✦ —

Brendan Phibbs MD became a cardiologist. He started Tucson's first mobile cardiac-care unit and traveled many times to the Tohono O'odham and Navajo reservations, where he held free cardiology clinics. He led a crusade against silicosis and lung cancer among miners, resulting in the implementation of industry-wide health standards to protect the workers. He died at the ripe old age of 99.

— ✦ —

Jacques Lusseyran survived Buchenwald despite his blindness. He later became a lecturer in the United States. His remarkably optimistic *Et la lumière fut* became the source and template for Anthony Doerr's award-winning novel *All the Light We Cannot See*.

— ✦ —

Descended from one of Scotland's most distinguished aristocratic families, the tall and striking **Clementine Churchill** backed out of two engagements before accepting marriage to Winston Churchill, who had instantly detected in her 'so much intellectual quality'. By inclination, Clementine was a Liberal rather than a Tory, with a good understanding of local politics. During the war, Churchill made her privy to the Ultra secrets.

One of her main achievements was to have utterly charmed influential Americans in London when England was on its own, such as the broadcast journalist Ed Murrow and other people with direct access to President Roosevelt in the White House. She organized many small dinners at Downing Street to help cement Anglo-American ties. She also discreetly kept files on her guests' favorite dishes to serve them 'ambrosial' meals.

— ◆ —

Svetlana Alliluyeva was reunited with Alexei Kapler eleven years after their abrupt separation. They were soon secret lovers and vacationed together on the shore of the Black Sea, even though he had married shortly before being released from a labor camp. Her reputation as Stalin's rebellious daughter took another turn when she converted to the Russian Orthodox faith in 1962.

During a trip to India, Svetlana defected to the West, a major propaganda blow to the Soviet Union. For a while she settled in Scottsdale, Arizona, and in the early 1980s moved with her daughter to Cambridge in England, where she converted to the Roman Catholic Church. Two years later, she returned to the USSR to be reunited with her two Russian children. In her final years, she shuttled between England and Wisconsin.

February

By the time the three world leaders were meeting at Yalta in February 1945, the glue of mutual trust between FDR,

Churchill, and **Joseph Stalin** was fast dissolving. Until his death in April 1945, FDR believed that he could build a special relationship with the Soviet leader. Stalin's repressive policies in 1945 led to the division of Germany and Europe, symbolized by the Iron Curtain.

Stalin died in March 1953 and was soon denounced by Nikita Khrushchev in his 'Secret Speech' at the 20th Party Congress. Nevertheless, Vladimir Putin rehabilitated Stalin's image as the architect of Soviet power.

— ◆ —

Back home in the USA, **American and Filipino nurses** (also known as Angels of Bataan and Corregidor) benefitted from glamorous Hollywood publicity that romanticized and trivialized their ordeal. An attempt was made to obtain the Distinguished Service Medal for the chief nurse, but she only obtained the less-prestigious Legion of Merit. Apparently, her position lacked the exercising of independent initiative and responsibility necessary for achieving such an award. The nurses kept in touch and met as a group one last time, touring the Pentagon and visiting graveyards together in 1992. Nurse **Ruby Bradley** returned for service in Korea and in due time became the most decorated woman in American military history.

— ◆ —

Lea and **Virginia Gattegno** were part of the distinguished Luzzatto dynasty of Venice. Growing up in the Dodecanese Island of Rhodes, where their father was headmaster, the two sisters were self-educated at home when Mussolini's 1938 racial laws forbade them to attend school. After the war, the two sisters traveled to Rome where they worked in hospitals and orphanages. Within a year or two, Virginia married and settled on the Lido Island in Venice, while Lea eventually passed a foreign service examination in Rome in the early 1960s to take part in the new project of the European Community.

The two sisters remained inseparable, spending every summer together in Venice. Lea turned into an avid reader, while her sister liked to collect jazz records. Their cousin became the head of the Italian Jewish community. Both sisters gave lengthy taped interviews on their ordeal at Auschwitz-Birkenau.

— ✦ —

Alexander Isayevich Solzhenitsyn burst onto the world stage in 1962 with the publication of his *A Day in the Life of Ivan Denisovich*. He had spent eight years in the labor camp system and survived undiagnosed cancer in Kazakhstan. For his *Gulag Archipelago*, he secretly gathered testimonies from scores of former zeks. Surrounded by a tightly knit group of dedicated and capable, if invisible, women, Solzhenitsyn won the Nobel Prize for Literature in 1970 but could not travel to Stockholm at the time to receive the prize.

Solzhenitsyn was arrested and deported in 1974, eventually settling in remote Cavendish, Vermont. He returned to Russia in 1994, happy to see his work on primetime Russian television.

— ✦ —

Nearly a third of all US Marines killed in the Second World War died in Iwo Jima. The inspiring **Jack Rosenthal** picture appeared on the Seventh War Loan Bond and raised $26 billion in just three months.

Three of the flag-raisers died, while the three others returned to the USA and were reassigned to 'civilian morale duty' with the war bond tour. They shook hands with the president in front of the cameras, raised their flag over the Capitol once more, and appeared at a midday crush of spectators on Times Square.

Among the three survivors, Ira Hayes, a soft-spoken Pima Indian from Arizona who was affectionately known as 'Chief', felt deep inner misgivings. Hayes started to rail against the hoopla, the phoniness, the steak dinners, and loudmouths shoving drinks in his hands. As his comments started to give offence, he had to be pulled out from the tour.

Inspired by the famous flag-raising picture, the US Marine Corps dedicated a large bronze memorial in 1954 on the flank of Arlington National Cemetery, honoring all Marines who have died in the defense of the United States since 1775. The movie *Sands of Iwo Jima* turned John Wayne into a Hollywood star.

— ◆ —

Pablo Picasso remains perhaps the most famous twentieth-century painter, playing a key role in the image of the modern artist. Picasso's irrepressible artistic searches demonstrated that one never needed to cling to merely one style of artistry, e.g., his blue period, rose period, primitivism, cubism, analytical cubism, synthetic cubism. Although painting was his principal medium, his sculptures, ceramics, prints, papiers collés, and theater designs were also widely celebrated.

Details of his personal life from the 1930s onward were widely circulated, not unlike rock stars in our contemporary world. His 'virile behavior' toward women swung between wild bohemian stereotypes and essentially bourgeois values. To be sure, his work was often caricatured and misunderstood in many art schools. The 1985 opening of the Musée Picasso in Paris marked the beginning of a more nuanced approach to his complex legacy.

— ✦ —

Simone de Beauvoir was to become one of the central figures in left-wing French intellectual circles in the post-war period. In 1949, she published *Le Sexe Second*, exploring the historical and societal construction of women as the 'Other' in a male-dominated world. Gender roles were not innate but socially constructed. Published in 1953 in the United States, *The Second Sex* sold more than 1 million paperback copies.

During the Algerian War of Independence, Simone de Beauvoir took up the legal case of Djamila Boupacha to publicize rape as a weapon of war. In April 1971, she signed the 'Manifesto of the 343', published in the weekly *Le Nouvel Observateur*, advocating for reproductive rights.

One of her most enduring legacies remains her four-volume autobiography: *Memoirs of a Dutiful Daughter* (1958), *Force of Circumstance* (1963), *The Coming of Age* (1972), and *All Said and Done* (1974).

March

In the United States and in England, distinguished publishing houses such as Alfred A. Knopf and Secker & Warburg initially rejected **Anne Frank's** diary, calling it 'dull'. Doubleday bought the rights after a young assistant by the name of Judy Jones in Paris saw the lovely face of Anne on the cover of the French edition.

The Anne Frank Museum opened in 1960, providing an unforgettable experience for children to see the annex with their own eyes. Translated into sixty languages, the diary became a totemic book for inquisitive teenagers around the world.

— ✦ —

Long before the US Supreme Court's 1967 *Loving vs Virginia* landmark civil rights case, striking down laws banning inter-racial marriage, **Elinor Powell** and **Frederick Albert** faced much animosity. In April 1946, the two made love in the hope of conceiving a child.

After being shipped back to Europe, Frederick learned of his son's birth through a Western Union Telegram: 'Eight-pound son born December eighteenth. Mother child well. Gladys Powell.'

After marrying in New York in 1947, the pair experienced unremitting prejudice. They left for Germany in 1952, where their mixed-race child (*Mischlingskind*) faced another type of ostracism. They returned to the United States, where he became vice president at Pepperidge Farm.

— ✦ —

Like many photographers of her generation, **Margaret Bourke-White** was drawn to the geometric scales of archi-tecture and industry, visiting factories to catch improbable angles. The FBI closely monitored her whereabouts during the Red Scare in the late 1940s.

One of the highlights of her career was to join *Life* maga-zine, where she worked almost without interruption until 1957. She traveled to India and photographed Mahatma Gandhi hours before his assassination. She also visited South African gold mines and Korea. Her twenty-year struggle with Parkinson's disease became a motion picture, *Double Exposure* (1989), featuring Farrah Fawcett as the intrepid photographer.

— ✦ —

Alfred Kinsey and **Clara Bracken McMillen** carried out groundbreaking research together. Their *Sexual Behavior in the*

Human Male (1948) and *Sexual Behavior in the Human Female* (1953) ushered in a new era of frank discussions. The second book, on aspects of female sexuality, sold less well than the first work – it was admittedly published the same year *Playboy* magazine hit the newsstand. The data on female masturbation and relationships outside marriage were often denounced as 'a Godless assault on the family and America'.

The counterculture of the 1960s gave America *Everything You Always Wanted to Know about Sex, but Were Afraid to Ask* (1969), followed by the search for peak experiences in *The Joy of Sex* (1972), *The Joy of Gay Sex* (1977), and *The Joy of Lesbian Sex* (1977). Later, the reassuring voice of Ruth Westheimer, a Jewish grandmother with a PhD from Columbia University, started to defend the virtues of marriage on WYNF Radio in New York.

— ✦ —

Baron Phillipe de Rothschild's multifaceted life earned him many honors and accolades. He commissioned artists to design labels for each vintage of Mouton Rothschild wine, starting with 'V' for Victory for the 1945 label. The elevation from Deuxième Cru ('second growth') to Premier Cru ('first growth') remains one of his finest achievements. In 1973, he collaborated with the American winemaker Robert Mondavi, establishing the Opus One winery in Napa Valley and broadening the appeal of the Rothschild brand. Baron Philippe is remembered for his generous support for the arts and his role in cultural circles in Paris and New York.

April

A born tinkerer, **John Cage** was drawn to all manner of percussion, later espousing Eastern philosophies. He arrived in New York penniless during the war, befriended John Steinbeck, and roomed at Peggy Guggenheim's. The exceptional dancer/choreographer association lasted four decades. Twenty-six-year-old John Cage met the 19-year-old **Merce Cunningham** at the Cornish School in Seattle where he taught in 1938. Cunningham was drawn to Cage's brainy imagination during percussion group sessions. 'You were playing everything absolutely perfectly. Now go a little further and make a few mistakes.'

Cage divorced his wife, Xenia, in 1946 and he and Merce quietly lived together as a couple in New York from then on.

— ✦ —

Not much is known about the Kamikaze pilot **Hayashi Ishizo**. His mother and sister published his letters to emphasize the pointless sacrifice and dreadful hypocrisy among elderly Japanese commanders and ministers.

— ✦ —

Franklin Delano Roosevelt won a record four terms in office. After his death, a steady stream of books would praise this epochal leader who turned the USA into a superpower and launched many welfare programs. Indeed, FDR considerably extended the reach of the Federal Government and American might. His death in the spring of 1945 coincided with the time the United Nations delegates drafted the charter in San Francisco. Reaganomics, in due time, challenged the wisdom of FDR's Keynesian deficit spending to stimulate the economy, advocating tax cuts for the wealthy.

— ✦ —

Born and raised in Indochina, **Marguerite Duras** had returned to metropolitan France before the war to complete a law degree. Her husband, Robert Anthelme, was deported to the Dachau concentration camp and returned in very poor health. Marguerite became a prominent member of the Left Bank intelligentsia. Her novel *The Lover* was turned into a hit movie later in her life.

— ✦ —

The son of a wealthy businessman, **John F. Kennedy** could have lived the life of a playboy. Elected to the House of Representatives in 1952 and to the Senate in 1958, Kennedy went on to win one of the closest presidential elections in US history against Richard Nixon. JFK embodied an ethereal combination of youth, grace, and self-effacement, which played well on television. He was often plagued by excruciating pain in his lower back, leading to frequent hospitalizations.

After the CIA-backed Bay of Pigs fiasco in Cuba, which failed to overthrow Castro's new Communist regime, JFK went on TV to assume full responsibility. During the Cuban Missile Crisis, he opted for a cautious, wait-and-see embargo policy. Before his assassination in Dallas, JFK proposed the Peace Corps and the Apollo space program.

— ✦ —

Bernd Freytag von Loringhoven swam across rivers and spent a day in a ditch as Russians combed through the woods with dogs. Swapping his uniform for workers' old clothes, he made desperate efforts to get out of the Russian zone of occupation. On the advice of a German diplomat, von Loringhoven revealed his identity and was interrogated by British staff officers.

He vehemently insisted that there was a clear division between the Nazi Party and the Wehrmacht, denying any knowledge of concentration camps. After two and a half years of captivity, he was set free. When Germany became a member of NATO in 1955 and the Bundeswehr was formed, he went back into uniform.

May

Vasily Grossman died in obscurity in 1964, although he had been one of Russia's most popular war reporters. After Stalin's death in 1953, he wrote large sections of his masterpiece *Zhizn i Sudba* (*Life and Fate*), which the KGB confiscated, including the carbon copies and earlier drafts. During a meeting with the party's chief ideology guardian Mikhail Suslov, Grossman was told that his novel would be published in 250 years – a roundabout compliment. Fortunately, satirical writer Vladimir Voinovich and nuclear scientist Andrei Sakharov each owned a copy. The manuscript was anonymously smuggled out to Switzerland in 1980. In *Life and Fate*, the protagonist Anna Strum writes an immortal mother-to-son love letter from the ghetto while she is expecting imminent death.

— ◆ —

A First World War hero and early member of the Nazi Party, **Hermann Göring** was for a long time Hitler's designated successor. The rank of Reichsmarschall was created for him after the Luftwaffe's victories in the summer of 1940. Göring next promised Hitler that the German Air Force alone could bring England to its knees, but instead of prioritizing the destruction of RAF runways, Göring focused on bombing London, dragging Germany into a fatal two-front war.

Göring's drug addictions, indolence, vanity, economic mismanagement, and thirst for looted art made him many enemies. Nevertheless, during the Nuremberg Trials, Göring showed fighting spirit, embarrassing Robert Jackson during cross-examination. He cheated the gallows by swallowing a cyanide pill just hours before he was due to be executed.

— ✦ —

J.D. Salinger belonged to the post-Second World War renaissance of American literature. Unlike many of his Jewish contemporaries, the author retreated to the countryside in New Hampshire to live the life of a hermit. Shunning the adult world, its hierarchies and hypocrisies, Salinger blocked many attempts to write his biography. He believed that the artist was the only true seer we have on earth. The root of all evil was Western-style logic or ends–means analyses by higher ups. In the story 'Teddy', Salinger explains himself:

> You know that apple that Adam ate in the Garden of Eden? You know what was in that apple? ... Logic. Logic and intellectual stuff. That was all that was in it. So – this is my point – what you have to do is vomit it up if you want to see things as they really are.

— ✦ —

Hitler's favorite architect and wartime Minister of Armaments and War Production **Albert Speer** was lucky not to be hanged at the Nuremberg Trials. One reason is that he was the only Nazi leader to admit his guilt. During his twenty-year stint in the Spandau Prison (in the British sector of Western Berlin), he read voraciously and secretly transmitted letters to his children. He also ordered guidebooks so that he could imagine walking from place to place, traveling through southern Siberia, crossing the Bering Straits, and ending his journey in Guadalajara, Mexico. In 1970, he published *Inside the Third Reich*, exaggerating his role to revive the German war economy, downplaying his commitment to the Nazi cause, and insisting that he had no knowledge of the Holocaust.

June

Pierre Bonnard started painting subjects that were in a bathtub from 1925 onward. In 1937, he admitted to a Swedish journalist that nudes and bathroom scenes, with their close-packed compositional geometry, were breathtakingly difficult. The close-up views, the spatial arrangements, the confinement of the body, the matte colors of the enamel and the reflected light on the grid pattern of tiles clearly fascinated him. Whereas impressionists celebrated *plein-air* painting, Bonnard praised the innocent banality and chromatic refinement, harmonic splendor, and multifaceted reflections of his own home.

— ◆ —

After close to five years of captivity, **Major Siegfried Knappe** returned home in 1949. He immigrated with his family to the United States and settled in Ohio. Thanks to his memoirs, he appeared as an adjutant to General Weidling in the movie *Downfall* (2004), narrating the last days of dictator Adolf Hitler in his bunker in Berlin.

— ◆ —

Former **Land Girls** dispersed after the war. Between 1996 and 1999 historians went in search of these 'invisible' women to highlight their significant contribution to New Zealand's war effort. Historians put together successive alphabetical lists, having to overcome difficulties with married names. The historians then conducted systematic oral history interviews of the Women's Land Service (2,711 Land Girls), every so often confused and mixed up with those who served in the WAAC (2,008), WRNS (501), and WAAF (2,541). The interviews detailing enterprise and resourcefulness were carefully transcribed for posterity. What also survives are nostalgic photographs of young women in full bloom.

July

Lee Miller modeled for the most notable photographers of the day, including Edward Steichen, Horst P. Horst, and Man Ray, before deciding to work behind the camera. She worked for American and British *Vogue*. Picasso painted her portrait. She produced her own art, while surrealists chopped up her beautiful features.

In the 1 April 1945 issue of the American *Vogue*, she commented on 'G.I. Lingo in Europe', writing, 'Now we "liberate" a bottle of brandy when we beat down a mercenary publican, we "liberate" a girl when we detach her from her chaperone.'

— ✦ —

Hemingway, Shaw, Remarque, Cocteau, and Malraux, not to mention hundreds of reporters, at one moment or another paid tribute to **Marlene Dietrich**. In turn, she was touched by the dedication and innocence of very young American soldiers sacrificing their lives for the sake of freedom. For many years after the war, she led the life of a vagabond, eventually settling in Paris. Fiercely protective of her privacy, visitors to her apartment on Avenue

Montaigne were often struck by a telephone ringing interminably in another room. When she passed away in 1992, her coffin was draped in an American flag and flown to reunited Berlin.

— ✦ —

During the war, **Robert Jackson** had dissented from the court's majority in *Korematsu vs United States*, which focused on transplanted American citizens and principles of racial discrimination. When visiting Lauterpacht in Cambridge, Jackson wanted to place the individual person as an appropriate subject of international law, but how? At the time, international law only dealt with sovereign states. One way to bypass this difficulty might be to focus on large criminal organizations, such as the SS. Jackson made every effort to uphold the majesty of the law as he pushed forward the novel concept of 'crimes against humanity'. Prosecutor and law professor Telford Taylor called his opening statement at the Nuremberg Trials the 'Big Bang' of international law.

— ✦ —

Trained in piano in the Mount Zion Baptist Church in Newark from the age of 7, **Sarah Vaughan** also developed a remarkable talent as a singer. In 1947, she won the *Esquire* magazine New Star Award and by the 1950s had gained an international following. Vaughan is known for listening for hours to records to find the point of inflection that suited her to 'lift' melodies from chord structures, taking apart and reconstructing popularly acclaimed songs with unmatched sweetness, flexibility, and purity. This she achieved through extraordinary breath control and idiosyncratic legato phrasing. In a way, her peculiar gift was to bring secular and sacred music closer together, or, in other words, closer to heaven.

— ✦ —

Winston Churchill found it hard to believe that he had been beaten by the bland Labour leader Clement Attlee. The Labour Party victory owed much to the Beveridge Report, which promised universal protection from poverty through a financial safety net. Out of office, Churchill embarked on his six-volume history, *The Second World War* (1948–53), for which he received the Nobel Prize for Literature in 1953. Aided by research assistants and with privileged access to confidential government papers, Churchill synthesized a wealth of material but also selectively omitted several key points, such as the Katyn Forest massacre and the failure to bomb Auschwitz.

Churchill returned to office as prime minister in 1951. Much weakened by a stroke, he decided to resign in 1955. He lived for another ten years, sharing some of his rich wisdom with the young monarch Elizabeth II. Churchill's dogged leadership, his wry sense of humor, his eloquent prose and memorable radio broadcasts remain without equal in the twentieth century.

— ✦ —

After a stint as Minister of Information and Broadcasting, **Indira Gandhi** became Prime Minister of India from 1966 to 1977. She is best remembered for the Green Revolution, and the nationalization of the commanding heights of the economy, as well as a controversial State of Emergency in 1975. After her defeat in 1977, she rebuilt her political base and staged a political comeback three years later. In 1984, her Sikh bodyguards assassinated her in retaliation for Operation Blue Star, a military operation which had removed Sikh militants from the Golden Temple in Amritsar.

August

From afar, the mushroom cloud was visible for an hour and a half. *Enola Gay* was almost 400 miles away when Bob Caron, the tail-gunner, reported that the cloud could no longer be seen. A large reception committee welcomed the plane, which had taken off twelve hours before. The heroes piled into Jeeps to be debriefed in the Quonset hut that housed the Officers' Club of the 509th, with plenty of bourbon and lemonade on the tables.

The interviewers were skeptical of the size of the mushroom, convinced that the men were exaggerating when they said the whole city had been instantly obliterated from sight. The obsession with scientific precision was such that it drew nervous laughter from the airmen. The drop was scheduled for 9.15. 'Dutch, what time was the drop made?'

Consulting his log, Dutch replied, 'At 9.15.17 K.' This indicated seventeen seconds after 9.15 a.m.

'Why were you late?' the questioner asked with a straight face.

Hearing the unbelievable news, American troops in the Pacific celebrated wildly in the vast area they controlled. The atomic bomb remains the best-kept secret of the war, possibly the best-kept military secret of all time, with over 100,000 people working on the Manhattan Project.

— ◆ —

By 1945, an atmosphere of expectation has developed around **Jackson Pollock's** work. Critics, however, could not agree whether the violence and the lack of coherence they saw in his art was an asset or a liability. They quibbled about the 'gaping holes'. The public, however, responded in a visceral manner.

The 'angry' painter was lucky to be adopted during the war by Peggy Guggenheim, who organized solo shows for him. She lent him $2,000 to buy a ramshackle farmhouse in Springs, half a dozen miles from East Hampton. Pollock moved into the farmhouse in November 1945 with Lee Krasner, whom he had married a month earlier. The greater privacy set in motion stylistic experiments, such as the 'drip' technique which initially earned him the nickname 'Jack the Dripper'.

— ✦ —

In January 1989, the 124th Emperor of Japan, **Hirohito**, was lucky to die in his sleep at the age of 87 after a reign of sixty-two years. The last of the Second World War leaders, it was in his name that Japan launched its attack on Pearl Harbor in 1941, and it was by his order that Japan accepted unconditional surrender in 1945. In the post-war period, Hirohito presided over unprecedented boom years, promoting international friendship through the 1964 Olympics and the 1970 Osaka World Exposition.

He became the first Japanese emperor to leave Japan, meeting Richard Nixon in Anchorage, Alaska, as he and Empress Nagako traveled to Europe. A few years later, he visited the United States, hobnobbed with Hollywood stars, and at Disneyland shocked many Japanese TV viewers when he was seen shaking hands with ordinary Americans.

— ✦ —

Spurred by religious traditions or philosophical beliefs, American conscientious objectors defied government orders and societal expectations. After the war, the costs of non-conformity were high in that those who had sought alternatives to military service, often working in psychiatric wards, were denied the largesse of the GI Bill. Conscientious objectors jumpstarted the Puerto Rico health service, where they were welcomed with open arms. John Kellam, **Carol Zens Kellam's** husband, was released in 1946.

— ✦ —

Josip Broz Tito spent the first years of the post-war period hunting down 'enemies of the state'. The repressions continued after the Stalin–Tito split of 1948 when Yugoslav Communists were rooted out as 'Cominformists'. Tito famously initiated socialist self-management in the form of producers' and consumers' co-ops, a curious cross between capitalism and Soviet planning.

His long journey to find the right female companion ended in 1952, after an operation for gallstones. Tito decided to marry Jovanka Budisavljević, who had nursed him back to health. She also happened to be one of his favorite cooks.

In 1961, Yugoslavia became a founding member of the Non-Aligned Movement. To increase his bargaining power between East and West, Tito travelled widely to meet foreign leaders. Meanwhile, virtually every town and region of Yugoslavia showered the triumphant leader with gleaming new villas and hunting lodges.

— ✦ —

Backed up by peasants and guerilla tactics, **Mao Zedong** went on to defeat the National Revolutionary Party, which retreated to Taiwan. He proclaimed the People's Republic of China in October 1949. Communists now ruled one-third of the world's population.

To release labor for industry, he unleashed the Great Leap Forward (1958–60), bundling small collective farms into huge communes. This unmitigated economic disaster led to the century's most devastating famine, with approximately 45 million deaths. To consolidate his power, Mao cheered the Cultural Revolution (1966–76) to purge Chinese society of 'bourgeois' influence. Red Guards terrorized government and party leaders, and scholars were exiled to the countryside. For ten long years, priceless art was destroyed and irreplaceable first editions were burned. Western biographies of Mao are still blocked on mainland China.

— ✦ —

Maria Klimoff's desperate attempts to move her family to a safer place was a common occurrence in 1945. Her family spent four years in Bavaria, then moved to Canada. Her son, Alexis Klimoff, became a Professor of Russian Literature at Vassar College and a close friend of Alexander Solzhenitsyn.

September

Ho Chi Minh's Declaration of Independence can be described as the first day of a thirty-year war. The founder and first leader of the Vietnamese nationalist movement, Ho Chi Minh ('Bringer of Light') presided over North Vietnam from 1954 to 1969. Together with General Giap, he defeated the French at the Battle of Dien Bien Phu in 1954. At the Geneva Peace talks, Vietnam was divided into the communist north (of the 17th Parallel), and non-communist south. Nevertheless, Ho was determined to reunite his country, even if this meant clashing with the United States, his initial ally against the French.

Although 'Uncle Ho' was widely viewed as the Father of the Nation, the Politburo sidelined and silenced him in the second half of the Vietnam War. He died of heart failure in 1969, like many twentieth-century statesmen refusing to stop chain-smoking (American-made Salems). It would take another six years for the USA to withdraw from Vietnam.

Generally described as courtly, urbane, highly sophisticated, and remarkably friendly (*New York Times* obituary), Ho was reluctant to disclose biographical information. Relying on a dozen or so aliases in his underground years, details on his family, revolutionary ideals, and loves remain elusive.

— ✦ —

As Supreme Commander of the Allied powers, **General MacArthur** displayed mercy and magnanimity to temper one of the most authoritarian societies in the world. Building solid ties with Emperor Hirohito, he put the Japanese back to work, drafted a liberal constitution that gave women the right to vote, imposed land reform, and facilitated the rise of a free press. MacArthur fell afoul of President Truman when he started behaving like a vainglorious military figure bent on commandeering civilian power. One of his last acts was to save Korea from being overrun. He was perhaps the 'last American hero', although he threatened to use the atomic bomb against China – certainly not a courageous virtue.

— ✦ —

Lord Mountbatten was a close relative of the royal family. Serving as the Viceroy in India in 1947, he failed to persuade Hindus and Muslims of the benefits of unity. He achieved his lifelong dream when he served his final posting at the Admiralty as First Sea Lord (1955–59). In retirement, Mountbatten helped to raise funds for the United World Colleges and pleaded eloquently for arms control. In August 1979, the Irish Republican Army (IRA) detonated a bomb as he was out in a fishing boat to collect lobster pots, killing him instantly.

— ✦ —

Dame Edwina Mountbatten (née Ashley) inherited the immense Cassel fortune in 1921. The Second World War turned Edwina Mountbatten into a leading member of the Red Cross and the Order of St John. She was a brilliant administrator and indefatigable visitor of shelters and hospitals. In the wake of the Japanese surrender, she gathered rescue teams to locate and rescue British POWs who were scattered in numerous camps over a vast territory. During the partition of India, she co-ordinated the work of major voluntary organizations to help save desperate refugees. During these trying times she drew close to Jawaharlal Nehru, the future Prime Minister of India. The two remained in touch during the next twelve years. When she passed away in 1960, she was buried at sea with naval honors, with Nehru ordering an Indian warship to escort the ceremony off Portsmouth.

— ✦ —

In 1948, **Nelson Mandela** witnessed the rise of apartheid which served the interests of a white minority. The stark 'divide and rule' programs kept other races poor and uneducated, imposed a strict internal passport system, and sexual relationships between whites and non-whites were banned. He opened South Africa's first black law practice in 1952.

In response to the Sharpeville Massacres of March 1961, Mandela founded the ANC's armed wing. Arrested and put on trial, Mandela narrowly escaped the death penalty, thanks to a formidable defense team with ties to London. On Robben Island, Mandela proved himself a disciplined and indefatigable spiritual leader.

One of his life's most momentous decisions in retrospect was to learn Afrikaans, the language of the oppressor. Sustained by the political strength of Zulu leader Buthelezi, the moral clarity of Desmond Tutu, and the passionate love of Winnie Mandela, he managed to stay in the news, thanks also partly to the rise of transistor radio, and later, CNN's global impact.

Following delicate consultations with the ANC leadership to renounce violence, Nelson Mandela embarked on a series of secret negotiations with President De Klerk. Both received the Noble Peace Prize in 1993. The following year, the ANC won the country's first free elections, and Mandela became South Africa's first black president in May 1994.

— ◆ —

Albert Camus grew up in Algeria. A former member of the Resistance, he published *The Plague* in 1947, which takes place in a city that is sealed off after an outbreak of bubonic plague, a byword for the deadly Nazi disease. The fundamental idea was that when the chips are down, people struggle in their own ways. The only cowardice is to get on your knees – i.e., fatalism. Camus went on to win the Nobel Prize. Despite his worldwide fame, he could do little to stop torture during the Algerian War of Independence. Nevertheless, he pleaded diplomatically with high-court judges and the French President not to impose the death penalty.

Flush with royalties from his acclaimed books, Camus was often approached for a loan. He was famously very generous. Camus' universe consisted of believing in God without clinging to immortality.

— ◆ —

Dawn Powell was a playwright, novelist, scriptwriter, and prolific short-story writer. Just before the Second World War, Scribner became her publisher, with the legendary Maxwell Perkins as her editor. She was recognized late in her life and rediscovered posthumously with a spectacular revival in the 1990s.

October

When in 1946, **Christian Dior** met the businessman M. Boussac, he took an instant liking to him and his surroundings – plenty of books, Empire furniture, a bronze racehorse, and a gouache of Rome on the wall. The following year, Maison Christian Dior opened at 30 Avenue Montaigne. The place had a tiny studio, a salon to show the dresses, a dressing room for the mannequins, an office, six small fitting rooms, and sixty workers all told. Dior's revolutionary 'New Look' instantly put French haute couture back on the map. Brilliant photographers such as Irving Penn contributed to the look of ultra-feminine silhouette. Dior hired Yves Saint Laurent as his assistant.

— ◆ —

Growing up in poverty, **Maria Eva Duarte** rose meteorically when in 1943 she met Colonel Juan D. Perón, a 49-year-old widower and a rising figure in Argentinian politics. Together, they became the champions of the *decamisados*, 'the shirtless'. When Colonel Perón returned to power, Eva set up aid offices in the Ministry of Labor and Social Welfare, welcoming needy visitors. The beautiful *presidenta* also gave rousing speeches on the radio and appeared on oversized posters.

In 1947, she pushed through a bill that gave women the right to vote. Financed by lottery and movie tickets, her gigantic foundation went on to build entire communities and sustained healthcare services, although large amounts were also funneled into Swiss bank accounts. Her book *The Purpose of My Life*, published in 1951, became compulsory reading in the schools. When 'Evita' Perón passed away in 1952, nearly 3 million people attended the elaborate state funeral in the streets of Buenos Aires.

— ✦ —

Chang Kia-ngau never managed to break the impasse with the Soviets. In March 1947, he was appointed Governor of the Bank of China, working on currency reform. After the Communist takeover, he moved to Los Angeles, teaching at Loyola University and becoming a senior research fellow at Stanford's Hoover Institution.

— ✦ —

Airey Neave played an important role in MI9, the agency responsible for 'ratlines', building channels to extricate shot-down RAF pilots from occupied Holland, Belgium, and France. After the Nuremberg Trials, Neave was elected Member of Parliament for Abingdon. Not getting along with Edward Heath, he became Margaret Thatcher's campaign manager.

Given his remarkable wartime pedigree, Neave always remained close to the intelligence establishment, handling the Northern Ireland portfolio with Unionist instincts in the Thatcher Government. On 30 March 1979, an Irish National Liberation Army bomb exploded under his car as he drove up the ramp of the House of Commons car park. With both legs blown off, he died in the hospital an hour later.

— ✦ —

In 1946, the US Supreme Court used the **Tomoyuki Yamashita** decision as a precedent, increasing the parameters of responsibility. Called 'command responsibility' and also known as 'superior responsibility', it referred to the duty to supervise subordinates, imposing liability on commanders for 'a wanton, immoral disregard of the action of subordinates amounting to acquiescence'. The doctrine of command accountability was added to the Geneva Conventions and applied to the trials of former Yugoslavia commanders, and was later adopted by the International Criminal Court.

— ✦ —

Art patron **Peggy Guggenheim** grew up in one of New York's most affluent and prominent families and lost her father in the 1912 *Titanic* disaster. On inheriting close to $0.5 million, she moved to Paris, leading a bohemian life. She discovered the power of visual arts and in 1938 opened her London gallery of modern art. Returning to Paris, she bought hundreds of modern artworks from impoverished artists and brought them back to the United States, almost singlehandedly turning New York into the new international art capital.

In 1946, she published *Out of this Century*, the first of her two memoirs recounting romantic encounters with avant-garde artists. In 1947, she bought a palazzo on the Grand Canal in Venice, setting the stage for the ever-growing Venice Biennale, in due time opening her home as a museum. Her *Confessions of an Art Addict* appeared in 1960.

November

In 1947, **Hugh Trevor-Roper** published *The Last Days of Hitler*, tracking down and interrogating survivors of Hitler's court to paint a vivid picture of the circumstances of Hitler's death. Teaching at Christ Church Oxford after the war, his favorite medium, besides entertaining book reviews in Sunday papers, turned out to be humorous letters to close friends and former students. In 1985, he was embroiled in the fake Hitler diary controversy, overconfidently mistaking the forgery for the genuine thing.

— ✦ —

Isaiah Berlin gained recognition as a political theorist and historian of ideas through a series of influential BBC radio programs. His *Two Concepts of Liberty* (1958) distinguished between 'negative' and 'positive' liberty. A specialist of Russian nineteenth-century thinkers and a prominent defender of liberal democracy, Berlin engaged in important Cold War debates on tolerance and pluralism, whereby it is sometimes tough to choose between incommensurable goods.

— ✦ —

One of Russia's most revered poets, praised for her lyrical depth and emotional complexity, **Anna Akhmatova** began to gain international recognition after Stalin passed away in March 1953. She suffered for years on end from her son's arrest and deportation to Gulag labor camps. Only after his release in 1956 during the Khruschev Thaw could she begin to breathe more easily. (Her husband, the poet Nikolai Gumilev had been executed in the interwar years.)

In 1964, Akhmatova was awarded the Etna-Taormina international poetry prize in Italy and Oxford University awarded her an honorary doctorate in 1965. Akhmatova's tight friendship with Boris Pasternak sustained the latter in his efforts to publish the subversive *Dr. Zhivago*.

— ✦ —

Georgia O'Keefe finalized the purchase of her house, a $4,000 tax-deductible gift to the Church, on 31 December 1945. It took three years to renovate it. She transformed the original corral into a big studio which felt like being outdoors. During the repair work, Georgia O'Keefe was in New York City settling the estate of Stieglitz.

O'Keefe soon started a vegetable and flower garden which gave her immense pleasure. 'There are lots of startling poppies along beside the lettuce – all different every morning – so delicate – and gay – My onion patch is round and about 15 feet across – a rose in the middle of it.' When she began a series of paintings inspired by the patio door, she confessed that she had bought the place because of that specific aesthetic challenge. Up to 1960, she painted approximately thirty variations of the patio. O'Keefe would generally spend her winters and spring in Abiquiu and summer and fall at Ghost Ranch.

— ✦ —

The Nuremberg Court set a precedent for war crimes, collaboration, and genocide trials. The principles and procedures of the International Military Tribunal were applied to another twelve US Military Tribunals in Germany between 1946 and 1949, such as the Medical Case, charging senior Nazi doctors, or the Einsatzgruppen Case, prosecuting members of mobile killing squads.

That said, survivors who were eager to remember and transmit what they had witnessed in death camps confronted a combination of incomprehension and indifference. The Italian publisher Mondadori initially rejected Primo Levi's masterpiece, *If This Is a Man*, which detailed his ordeal at Auschwitz.

In 1960, the State of Israel judged and hanged Adolf Eichmann. Israeli agents had tracked him down in Argentina and kidnapped him to bring him back to Jerusalem. From then on, the mass murder of Jews was no longer treated as either a function of totalitarianism or an outgrowth of fascism. The Holocaust entered humanity's consciousness through visual masterpieces such as Claude Lanzmann's lengthy documentary *Shoah*, and Spielberg's *Schindler's List*.

— ✦ —

The youngest of six children, **Anna Freud** became a psycho-analyst without getting a medical degree. Her interests led her to focus on children, charting their emotional development, elucidating their secret wishes, phobias, traumas, dreams, and nightmares, with the aim of grasping relationships with parents, siblings, and friends. She wrote papers on the classic modalities of transference, resistance, and free associations, all the while countering theories by her rival Melanie Klein, also the daughter of a Viennese physician. Only after Vienna expressed regrets about the shabby treatment of her father did she return to that city to attend a 1971 conference of the International Psychoanalytic Association.

— ✦ —

While massacres of civilian populations and mistreatment of prisoners of war surfaced at the Tokyo War Crimes Trials, the mass rapes in China and plight of **comfort women**, most noticeably in Korea, came to the world's attention only decades later. For a long time, they were derided in Japan as 'fabrications'.

December

Heinrich Harrer gained worldwide fame when his memoirs were turned into a movie by the same name, *Seven Years in Tibet* (1997), starring Brad Pitt.

— ✦ —

One of the greatest pianists of the twentieth century, **Sviatoslav Richter's** career took off in 1960 with his international debut in Finland and at Carnegie Hall that same year. His historic recordings of Schubert's 'Sonata in B-Flat major', Beethoven's 'Appassionata', and Rachmaninoff's 'Piano Concerto No. 2' stand the test of time. Richter categorically refused to engage in conversations on 'interpretation', a most elastic term. He also made regular appearances at the Salzburg Festival and the Aldeburgh Festival, collaborating with composer Benjamin Britten.

— ✦ —

Cellist and conductor **Mstislav 'Slava' Rostropovich** was a gifted teacher, a funny raconteur and, with his wife, soprano opera singer Galina Vishnevskaya, a steadfast friend to people in need. Immediately after the war, he stayed in touch with the disgraced and lonely Shostakovich, and in the 1970s, he offered his *dacha* to dissident Alexander Solzhenitsyn.

In 1978, the Soviet authorities revoked his and his wife's citizenship, and they were not allowed to return to the USSR. This led to a new career in the West. In 1991, at the age of 63, Rostropovich began his lifelong dream of recording all six of the Bach suites. The CDs and videos were released in 1995.

— ✦ —

Eleanor Roosevelt exuded a kind of elevated fairness which struck President Truman and foreign observers as remarkable. She was not beholden to nationalism and avoided getting embroiled in puerile ideological rifts. In 1946, she was elected chairperson of the United Nations Commission on Human Rights. One of her first decisions was to pick a small team of savvy specialists to draft an International Declaration of Human Rights.

She had a knack for courteously but firmly interrupting long-winded diplomats and protecting the good name of the United States. Eleanor Roosevelt and her team adapted the 1789 French *Declaration des Droits de l'Homme* to the twentieth century. This meant including women, colonial subjects, and stateless refugees, while also mentioning welfare rights. The General Assembly voted on the Universal Declaration with the full knowledge that it was not a binding document.

After this historic 1948 vote, human rights in international affairs entered a twenty-year eclipse during which human rights were likened to naïve idealism. The countries that abstained in 1948 were those of the Soviet sphere of influence (because of class), South Africa (because of race), and Saudi Arabia (because of women). By the end of the twentieth century, the Soviet system and South Africa had collapsed.

— ✦ —

Marilyn Monroe soon became a Hollywood legend. Made of love and lust, her incomparable destiny gave rise to myriad stories, most of them unconscious projections of post-war America. She was indeed an infinity of character and mystery, and everyone made up his or her own Marilyn:

> I knew I belonged to the public and the world – not because I was talented, or even beautiful, but because I had never belonged to anyone else. The public was the only family I had ever dreamed about. I didn't go into movies to make money. I wanted to become famous so that everyone would like me, and I'd be surrounded by love and affection.

— ✦ —

Robert Capa died tragically on 25 May 1954. He was on a foot patrol with French soldiers in Vietnam's Red River Delta when he stepped on a landmine while gathering pictures for *Life* magazine.

Born in Budapest and learning his trade in Berlin and Paris, Capa snapped epochal shots of the Spanish Civil War, Omaha Beach on D-Day, and the liberation of Paris. Shortly after the war, he co-founded Magnum Photos, one of the first photographic co-operatives, owned entirely by its members. He and Ingrid Bergman toyed with the idea of getting married, but Capa drank too much and traveled a lot. She hesitated to leave her husband and ruin her standing in Hollywood.

— ◆ —

Swedish actress **Ingrid Bergman** had starred in *Casablanca* (1942), one of the most iconic propaganda movies of all times. In her best-known role, she was torn between her love for irresistible Rick (Humphrey Bogart) and her marital duty toward underground hero Victor Laszlo (Paul Henreid). Her marriage to neorealist director Roberto Rossellini in May 1950 caused a scandal.

On the advice of her children, she wrote *My Story* (1980) to counter false rumors about her past. In her memoirs, she discussed how she was vilified in Hollywood, narrating the creative partnership behind *Stromboli* (1950) and *Journey to Italy* (1954). She regained the public's favor when she won a second Academy Award for *Anastasia* (1956). *My Story* remains an essential read to grasp the challenges faced by iconic actresses in twentieth-century history.

Notes

To avoid disrupting the flow of the narrative with references, all relevant sources are provided here.

JANUARY

Hartman: freezing weather – J. Ted Hartman, *Tank Driver* (Indiana, 2003), pp. 57–61.

Rudel: clean shirt – Hans-Ulrich Rudel, *Stuka Pilot* (New York, 1979), p. 226.

Kahlo: Frida Kahlo, *The Diary of Frida Kahlo* (New York, 1995), p. 274; Hayden Herrera, *Frida Kahlo: The Paintings* (New York, 1991), pp. 218, 226, 265; *pulqueria* and *lavadoria* – Malka Drucker, *Frida Kahlo* (New York, 1991), pp. 121–23; *jewelry* and *wardrobe* – Claire Wilcox & Circe Henestrosa, *Frida Kahlo: Making Herself Up* (London, 2018) pp. 84–113.

Wallenberg: trap door – Kati Marton, *Wallenberg* (New York, 1982), pp. 153–54.

Phibbs: expletives – Brendan Phibbs, *The Other Side of Time: A Combat Surgeon in World War II* (Boston 1987), p. 158; *short of novocaine* – ibid., p. 223.

Lusseyran: *'Marseillaise'* – Jacques Lusseyran, *Et la lumière fut* (Chatou, 1987), p. 377; *'bloc des invalides'* – ibid., pp. 391–92.

Churchill: *The Personal Letters of the Churchills*, edited by their daughter, Mary Soames (New York, 1998), pp. 510–12; Valletta Harbor – Winston S. Churchill, *Memoirs of the Second World War* (One volume edition, New York, 1978), p. 912; Crimea – Lord Moran, *Churchill at War, 1940–45* (London, 2002), pp. 264–65; lavish buffet – Edward Stettinius, *Roosevelt and the Russians* (Garden City, 1949), p. 80. See also, S.M. Plokhy, *Yalta: The Price of Peace* (Penguin, 2011), pp. 21, 37; Sarah Churchill, *Keep On Dancing* (London, 1981), p. 73; and John Meacham, *Franklin and Winston* (New York, 2003).

Svetlana: romance with Kapler – Simon Sebag Montefiore, *Stalin: The Court of the Red Tsar* (New York, 2004), pp. 393–96; Rosemary Sullivan, *The Extraordinary and Tumultuous Life of Stalin's Daughter* (New York, 2015); Kapler's love letter in *Pravda* – Beata de Robien, *La Malédiction de Svetlana* (Paris, 2016), p. 167.

February

Corregidor nurses: 'Hello, folks!' – Elizabeth M. Norman, *We Band of Angels: The Untold Story of American Nurses Trapped on Bataan by the Japanese* (New York, 1999), p. 203.

Lea and Virginia: Luzzatto (Luzzatti) dynasty – 1906 *Jewish Encyclopedia* (jewishencyclopedia.com); Lea's taped interview – Fondation Auschwitz / Fortunoff testimonies; Virginia's taped interview – Steven Spielberg USC Shoah Foundation; retirement – Hannah Roberts, 'Survivor's Story: Venetian Ghetto's Last Witness to Auschwitz', *Financial Times Weekend Edition*, 25 May 2016.

Solzhenitsyn: arrest – Alexander Solzhenitsyn, *The Gulag Archipelago*, Vol. 1 (London, 1982), p. 4; and *I wish you happiness, Captain Solzhenitsyn*, ibid., p. 19; Michael Scammel, *Solzhenitsyn* (London, 1986), pp. 142–43.

Iwo Jima: The Iwo Jima historiography is immense. See, esp. Karal Ann Marling & John Wetenhall, *Iwo Jima: Monuments, Memories, and the American Hero* (Cambridge, MA, 1991).

Picasso: *The Charnel House* – Serraller & Semprun, *Picasso: Tradition and Avant-Garde* (Exhibition catalogue, Madrid, 2006), p. 270; and Jean Leymarie, *Picasso: The Artist of the Century* (New York, 1972), p. 259; first reactions – Pierre Caizergues & Ioannis Kontaxopoulos, *Picasso / Cocteau: Correspondance, 1915–1963* (Paris, 2018).

de Beauvoir: border crossing – Simone de Beauvoir, *La Force des Choses* (Paris, 2018), p. 961.

March

Remagen: 'Quick-Thinking Yanks …', *The Washington Post*, 10 March 1945.

Valentina Kuzminichna Bratchikova-Borshchevskaya: 8 March – Svetlana Alexievich, *The Unwomanly Face of War: An Oral History of Women in World War II* (New York, 2017), pp. 171, 163.

Frank: diary entries – Ruud van der Rol & Rian Verhoeven, *Anne Franck: Beyond the Diary* (New York, 1993), p. 64.

Albert marriage proposal – Alexis Clark, *Enemies in Love: A German POW, a Black Nurse, and an Unlikely Romance* (New York, 2018), pp. 108–09.

Jennings: first steps – Jean Jennings Bartik, Jon T. Rickman & Kim D. Todd, *Pioneer Programmer: Jean Jennings Bartik and the Computer that Changed the World* (Kirksville, 2000).

Bourke-White: old man – Jonathan Silverman, *For the World to See: The Life of Margaret Bourke-White* (New York, 1983), p. 150.

Notes

Baron Philippe de Rothschild: kindly get out of my house – Joan
Littlewood & Baron Philippe de Rothschild, *The Autobiography of Philippe
de Rothschild* (London, 1984), p. 186; loyal staff – Herbert R. Lottman, *The
French Rothschilds* (New York, 1995), p. 255; French–German negotiations
– J.M. Dreyfus, *Pillages sur ordonnances* (Paris, 2003), pp. 214, 222; private
art collection theft – Niall Ferguson, *The House of Rothschild* (New York,
1999), pp. 477–78.

V-rockets: Vengeance weapons – Calvocoressi, Wint, & Pritchard,
The Penguin History of the Second World War (London, reprint 1999),
pp. 556–60.

APRIL

Stalin: paranoia – Simon Sebag Montefiore, *Stalin: The Court of the Red Tsar*
(New York, 2003), pp. 429–30.

Cage: success – Kenneth Silverman, *Begin Again: A Biography of John Cage*
(Evanston, 2012), p. 63.

Ichizō: yellow rose – Emiko Ohnuki-Tierney, *Kamikaze Diaries: Reflections of
Japanese Student Soldiers* (Chicago, 2006), p. 175. See also *Diary and Letters to
Mother* (1995).

FDR: a terrible pain – Jim Bishop, *FDR's Last Year* (New York, 1974); and
David B. Woolner, *The Last 100 Days* (New York, 2017).

Dimbleby: *Belsen* – www.bbc.co.uk/videos/c87z7p0j3g5o.

Eleanor: United Nations – Blanche Wiesen Cook, *Eleanor Roosevelt: The War
Years and after 1939–1962*, Vol. 3 (New York, 2016), pp. 542–45.

Duras: Stalag numbers – Marguerite Duras, 'The War', in Richard J.
Aldrich, *Witness to War* (New York, 2004), pp. 633–34.

JFK: Hearst Newspapers – Nigel Hamilton, *JFK: Reckless Youth* (New York,
1992), pp. 681, 693, 697; and Michael O'Brien, *John F. Kennedy* (New
York, 2005), p. 181.

Hitler: wedding – Jonathan Mayo & Emma Craigie, *Hitler's Last Day Minute
by Minute* (London, 2016); and Bernd Freytag Von Loringhoven, *In the
Bunker with Hitler* (London, 2007).

MAY

Grossman: Anthony Beevor and Luba Vinogradova (eds), *A Writer at War*
(New York, 2005).

Norwegian: Albert Jaern, *And Then Came the Liberators*, translated from the
Norwegian by Solveig Schavland, with an afterword by Kathleen Stokker.
Edited by Richard Quinney (Madison, WI, 2001). See also, Jens Chr
Hauge, *The Liberation of Norway* (Oslo, 1995), pp. 100–01.

Göring: Richard Overy, *Goering* (London, 1984).

Belgian: sleeping husband – Anne Somerhausen, *Written in Darkness: A Belgian Woman's Record of the Occupation 1940–1945* (New York, 1946) in Richard J. Aldrich, *Witness to War* (New York, 2004), pp. 645–46.

Salinger: tricky, dreary farce – Eberhard Alsen, *J.D. Salinger and the Nazis* (Madison, WI, 2018), p. 93.

Speer: 'Do you know where Speer is?' – Donald L. Miller, *Masters of the Air* (New York, 2006), p. 464; sometimes amused face – John Kenneth Galbraith, *A Life in Our Times* (Boston, 1981), p. 207. See also Dan Van der Vat, *The Good Nazi* (Boston, 1997).

Phibbs: *Guten Appetit!* – Brendan Phibbs, *The Other Side of Time: A Combat Surgeon in World War II* (Boston, 1987), p. 328.

JUNE

Bonnard: bathers – Timothy Hyman, *Bonnard* (London, 1998), p. 199; play of reflections – Fondation Beyeler, *Pierre Bonnard* (Basel, 2012), p. 118. See also, Suzanne Page (ed.), *Pierre Bonnard* (Paris, 2006), p. 228.

JULY

Miller: Becky E. Conekin, 'Lee Miller: Model, Photographer, and War Correspondent in *Vogue*, 1927–1953', in *Fashion Theory*, 10 (1) (2015), pp. 97–126.

Dietrich: pearl-handled revolver – Steven Bach, *Marlene Dietrich: Life and Legend* (New York, 1992), p. 291.

Lauterpacht: crimes against humanity – Philippe Sands, *East West Street* (New York, 2016), p. 113.

Vaughan: I'll play for you – Leslie Gourse, *Sassy: The Life of Sarah Vaughan* (New York, 1993), p. 66; on artistic bond between Count Basie and Sarah Vaughan, *Count Basie, Good Morning Blues: The Autobiography of Count Basie* (New York, 1985).

Churchill: Gestapo speech – Martin Gilbert, *Churchill: A Life*, p. 847. Simon Eden – William Manchester & Paul Reid, *The Last Lion* (Boston, 2012), p. 951.

Gandhi: Pupul Jayakar, *Indira Gandhi: A Biography* (New Delhi, 1992), pp. 128–29.

AUGUST

Hiroshima: countdown – Joseph L. Marx, *Seven Hours to Zero* (New York, 1967), pp. 164–69; a dud? – Gustave Niebuhr, 'Hiroshima: Enola Gay's Crew Recalls the Flight into a New Era', *New York Times*, 6 August 1995; debriefing – Paul W. Tibbets, *Mission: Hiroshima* (New York, 1985), pp. 231–32. See also, John Hersey, 'Hiroshima', *The New Yorker*, 31 August 1946.

Pollock: strange, garbled news – Steven Naifeh & Gregory White Smith, *Jackson Pollock: An American Saga* (New York, 1989), p. 500; tiny summer place – *ibid.*, p. 499; initial reactions – B.H. Friedman, *Jackson Pollock: Energy Made Visible* (New York, 1964), pp. 76, 78; Jack the Dripper – Claude Cernucci, *Jackson Pollock: Meaning and Significance* (New York, 1992), p. 114.

Hirohito: surrender speech – Edward Behr, *Hirohito: Behind the Myth* (London, 1989), pp. 407–09. See also, Akira Kurosawa, *Something Like an Autobiography* (New York, 1982); Robert Guillain, *I Saw Tokyo Burning* (Garden City, New York, 1981).

Carol Zens Kellam: 11 August 1945 letter – Rachel Waltner Goossen, *Women against the Good War* (Chapel Hill, 1997), p. 114, quoted in Litoff & Smith (eds), *Since You Went Away*, p. 227.

Tito: 'Yugoslavs not going Communist, Tito says', *New York Times*, 14 August 1945; stabbed in the back below his left arm with a long two-pronged lance – Jasper Ridley, *Tito* (London, 1994), p. 64; Tito must be captured alive – William Klinger & Denis Kuljiš, *Tito's Secret Empire: How the Maharaja of the Balkans Fooled the World* (Oxford, 2021), pp. 159–60; refugees – Jasper Ridley, *Tito* (London, 1994), pp. 254, 260; trigger-happy security guards – Richard West, *Tito and the Rise and Fall of Yugoslavia* (London, 1994), p. 198.

Perth: baby aloft – Anthony J. Baker & Lisa Jackson, *Fleeting Attraction: A Social History of American Servicemen in Western Australia during the Second World War* (Nedlands, 1996), p. 230.

Shinkolobwe: Susan Williams, *Spies in the Congo: America's Atomic Mission in World War II* (New York, 2016), p. 225.

Mao: flight to Chongqing – Ross Terrill, *Mao: A Biography* (Stanford, 1999), pp. 209–10; clown – *ibid.*, p. 206; on the need to finesse the CCP's image abroad – Philip Short, *Mao: A Life* (New York, 1999), pp. 399–401.

Klimoff: email exchanges with her son, Professor Emeritus Alexis Klimoff.

SEPTEMBER

Ho Chi Min: all men are created equal – Cecil B. Currey, *Victory at Any Cost: the Genius of Viet Nam's Gen. Vo Nguyen Giap* (Washington, 1997), p. 104; independence – Peter MacDonald, *Giap: The Victor in Vietnam* (New York, 1993), p. 61; Major Archimedes L.A. Patti – John Colvin, *Volcano Under Snow: Vo Nguyen Gap* (London, 1996), p. 20; demeanor – Pierre Brocheux, *Ho Chi Minh* (Paris, 2002), p. 135.

MacArthur: Robert Harvey, *American Shogun: MacArthur, Hirohito, and the American Duel with Japan* (London, 2006), pp. 310–12.

Aung Sang: sense of humor – Tom Driberg, *Ruling Passions* (London, 1977), p. 215; Churchill or a Wellington – Philip Ziegler, *Mountbatten* (London, 1985), p. 321.

Lady Mountbatten: Dear Cousin – Madeleine Masson, *Edwina: The Biography of the Countess Mountbatten of Burma* (London, 1958), p. 144; gratitude from POWs – Dennis Holman, *Lady Louis* (London, 1952), pp. 90–94. See also, Janet Morgan, *Edwina Mountbatten* (London, 1991).

Kiley: Bruce M. Stave & Michele Palmer with Leslie Frank, *Witnesses to Nuremberg* (New York, 1998).

Mandela: Nelson Mandela, *Long Walk to Freedom* (Boston, 1994); Martin Meredith, *Nelson Mandela* (New York, 2010); Peter Limb, *Nelson Mandela* (Westport, 2008); Walter & Albertina Sisulu, *In Our Lifetime* (London, 2003).

Camus: the absurd (death) – Albert Camus, *Oeuvres complètes*, Vol. II: *La Pléiade* (Paris, 2006), p. 1005.

Powell: 29 September 1945 entry, *The Diaries of Dawn Powell, 1931–1965* (South Royalton, VT, 1995).

October

Balmain: *Fairchild's Who's Who in Fashion*, edited by Josephine Ellis Watkins (New York, 1975), p. 17; plump, balding bachelor – Charlotte Sinclair, *Vogue on Christian Dior* (New York, 2014), p. 8; triumphant début – *ibid.*, p. 21; elaborate workmanship – *Dior by Dior: The Autobiography of Christian Dior*, translated by Antonia Fraser (London, 1957/2007), p. 8.

Perón: Alicia Dujovne Ortiz & Shawn Fields, *Eva Perón* (New York, 1996); Eva Perón, *My Mission in Life* (New York, 1953); Julie M. Taylor, *Eva Perón* (Chicago, 1979); Jill Hedges, *Evita* (London, 2017); Robert J. Alexander, *Juan Domingo Perón* (Boulder, CO, 1979).

Chang Kia-ngau: 17 October 1945 diary entry, in Donald G. Gillin & Ramon H. Myers (eds), translated by Dolores Zen, *Last Chance in Manchuria: The Diary of Chang Kia-ngau* (Stanford, 1989), p. 78.

Neave: just shove the bundles into the cells – Alex Neave, *On Trial at Nuremberg* (Boston, 1978), p. 55; Keitel's carpet slippers – *ibid.*, p. 190.

Guggenheim: costumes – John Bernard Myers, *Tracking the Marvelous: A Life in the New York Art Word* (New York, 1983), pp. 48–49; underwear – Jacqueline Bograd Weld, *Peggy: The Wayward Guggenheim* (New York, 1986), p. 340.

November

Yamashita: ordered, condoned – Philip Piccigallo, *The Japanese on Trial* (Austin, 1979), p. 50; unworthy of our traditions – David Bergamini, *Japan's Imperial Conspiracy* (New York, 1971), p. 1053. See also, Arnold Brackman, *The Other Nuremberg* (New York, 1987), p. 245; Yuma Totani, *Justice in Asia and the Pacific Region, 1945–1952* (Cambridge, 2015); and Annette Gordon-Reed, *Race on Trial* (Oxford, 2002).

Trevor-Roper: Adam Sisman, *An Honourable Englishman* (New York, 2010).

Akhmatova: this evening – Michael Ignatieff, *Isaiah Berlin: A Life* (New York, 1998), pp. 151–61.

Georgia O'Keefe: *Maria Chabot – Georgia O'Keeffe Correspondence 1941–1949*, edited by Barbara Buhler Lynes & Anne Paden (Santa Fe, 2003), p. 295.

Jackson: opening statement – Second Day, Wednesday, 11/21/1945, Part 04, in Trial of the Major War Criminals before the International Military Tribunal, Volume II. Proceedings: 11/14/1945–11/30/1945. See also, Telford Taylor, *The Anatomy of the Nuremberg Trials* (New York, 1992), p. 177.

Freud: Elisabeth Young-Bruehl, *Anna Freud* (New Haven, 2008).

Comfort Women: preserve the chastity – George Hicks, *The Comfort Women: Japan's Brutal Regime of Enforced Prostitution in the Second World War* (New York, 1994), p. 160.

Finnish boy: *Finnpojke* (Martti Kalervo Broström) – Sue Saffle (ed.), *To the Bomb and Back: Finnish War Children Tell their World War II Stories* (New York, 2015), pp. 34–38.

DECEMBER

Harrer: rarefied air – Heinrich Harrer, *Seven Years in Tibet* (New York, 1996), p. 114.

Rostropovich: Elizabeth Wilson, *Rostropovich* (Chicago, 2008).

Roosevelt: I am pleased to inform you – Steve Neal, *Eleanor and Harry: The Correspondence of Eleanor Roosevelt and Harry S. Truman* (New York, 2002), pp. 50–51; organizational ability – Tamara K. Hareven, *Eleanor Roosevelt, An American Conscience* (Chicago,1968), p. 190.

Monroe: ultimatum – Anthony Summers, *Goddess: The Secret Lives of Marilyn Monroe* (New York, 1985), p. 12; character – Maurice Zolotow, *Marilyn Monroe* (New York, 1990), p. 9; anxieties on ownership – Sarah Churchwell, *The Many Lives of Marilyn Monroe* (New York, 2004), p. 215.

Kochendoerfer: Garmisch – Violet Kochendoerfer, *One Woman's World War II* (Lexington, 1994).

Bergman: Paris – Ingrid Bergman, *My Story* (New York, 1980), p. 152; dinner – Kershaw, *Blood and Champagne*, p. 59 (fictionalized account). See also, Noah Isenberg, *We'll Always have Casablanca* (New York, 2017); and Michel Lefebvre Bernard Lebrun, *Robert Capa: The Paris Years, 1933–1954* (New York, 2012).

Bibliography

Aldrich, Richard J. (ed.), *Witness to War: Diaries of the Second World War in Europe and the Middle East* (London: Doubleday, 2004).

Alexander, Robert J., *Juan Domingo Perón* (Boulder, CO: Westview Press, 1979).

Alexievich, Svetlana, *The Unwomanly Face of War: An Oral History of Women in World War II* (New York: Random House, 2018).

Alliluyeva, Svetlana, *Twenty Letters to a Friend* (New York and Evanston: Harper & Row, 1967).

Alliluyeva, Svetlana, *Only One Year* (London: Hutchinson, 1969).

Alsen, Eberhard, *J.D. Salinger and the Nazis* (Madison: University of Wisconsin Press, 2018).

Anderson, Benedict R., *Java in a Time of Revolution: Occupation and Resistance, 1944–1946* (Ithaca: Cornell University Press, 1972).

Atkinson, Rick, *The Guns at Last Light: The War in Western Europe, 1944–1945* (London: Picador, 2013).

Bach, Steven, *Marlene Dietrich: Life and Legend* (New York: W. Morrow, 1992).

Baker, Anthony J., & Lisa Jackson, *Fleeting Attraction: A Social History of American Servicemen in Western Australia During the Second World War* (Nedlands: University of Western Australian Press, 1996).

Bardsley, Dianne, *The Land Girls: In a Man's World, 1939–1946* (Dunedin, NZ: University of Otago Press, 2000).

Bartov, Omer, *Hitler's Army: Soldiers, Nazis, and War in the Third Reich* (New York: Oxford University Press, 1992).

Bartov, Omer, *The Holocaust: Origins, Implementation, Aftermath* (London and New York: Routledge, 2000).

Batinić, Jelena, *Women and Yugoslav Partisans* (New York: Cambridge University Press, 2015).

Beauvoir, Simone de, *La Force des choses* (Paris: Gallimard, 2018).

Beevor, Anthony, *The Fall of Berlin 1945* (New York: Viking 2003).

Beevor, Anthony, & Luba Vinogradova (eds), *A Writer at War: Vasily Grossman with the Red Army, 1941–1945* (New York: Pantheon Books, 2005).

Beevor, Anthony, *Ardennes 1944: Hitler's Last Gamble* (New York: Viking, 2015).

Behr, Edward, *Hirohito: Behind the Myth* (London: Hamish Hamilton, 1989).

Béon, Yves (ed.), *Planet Dora: A Memoir of the Holocaust and the Birthplace of Space Age* (Boulder, CO: Westview Press, 1997).

Bergamini, David, *Japan's Imperial Conspiracy* (New York: Morrow, 1971).

Bergman, Ingrid, *My Story* (New York: Delacorte Press, 1980).

Bishop, Jim, *FDR's Last Year* (New York: W. Morrow, 1974).

Blair, Clair, *Hitler's U-Boat War: The Hunted 1942–1945* (New York: Random House, 1996).

Bohlen, Charles, *Witness to History* (New York: W.W. Norton, 1973).

Brackman, Arnold, *The Other Nuremberg* (New York: Morrow, 1987).

Brocheux, Pierre, *Hô Chi Minh: du révolutionnaire à l'icône* (Paris: Payot, 2002).

Buhler Lynes, Barbara, & Ann Paden, *Maria Chabot–Georgia O'Keeffe Correspondence 1941–1949* (Albuquerque, New Mexico: University of New Mexico Press, 2003).

Buhler Lynes, Barbara, & Judy Lopez Agapita, *Georgia O'Keeffe and Her Houses* (New York: Harry N. Abrams, 2012).

Burleigh, Michael, *The Third Reich: A New History* (New York: Hill and Wang, 2001).

Burleigh, Michael, *Small Wars, Faraway Places* (London: Pan, 2013).

Buruma, Ian, *Year Zero: A History of 1945* (New York: Penguin Press, 2013).

Caizergues, Pierre, & Ioannis Kontaxopoulos, *Correspondance 1915–1963: Picasso, Cocteau* (Paris: Gallimard, 2018).

Calvocoressi, Peter, Guy Wint, & John Pritchard, *The Penguin History of the Second World War* (London: Penguin, 1999).

Camus, Albert, *Oeuvres complètes*, Vol. II (Paris: Gallimard, 2006).

Cannadine, David (ed.), *Blood, Toil, Tears and Sweat: Winston Churchill's Famous Speeches* (London: Penguin Classics, 2007).

Cernucci, Claude, *Jackson Pollock: Meaning and Significance* (New York: Westview Press, 1992).

Churchill, Winston, *Memoirs of the Second World War* (New York: Houghton Mifflin, 1978).

Churchwell, Sarah, *The Many Lives of Marilyn Monroe* (New York: Picador, 2004).

Clark, Alexis, *Enemies in Love: A German POW, a Black Nurse, and an Unlikely Romance* (New York: The New Press, 2018).

Condon, Bill, *Kinsey: Public and Private* (New York: HarperCollins, 2004).

Davies, Norman, *Europe at War 1939–1945: No Simple Victory* (London: Macmillan, 2006).

Diamond Hanna, *Women in the Second World War in France, 1939–48: Choices and Constraints* (Harlow: Longman, 1999).

Dimbleby, Richard, *Belsen* (www.bbc.co.uk/videos/c87z7p0j3g5o).

Dior, Christian, *Dior by Dior: The Autobiography of Christian Dior*, trans. by Antonia Fraser (London: V&A Publishing, 2018).

Djilas, Milovan, *Wartime* (New York: Harcourt Brace Jovanovich, 1977).

Dower, John W., *Embracing Defeat: Japan in the Wake of World War II* (New York: W.W. Norton, 2000).

Dreyfus, Jean-Marc, *Pillages sur ordonnances: Aryanisation et restitution des banques en France 1940–1953* (Paris: Fayard, 2003).

Driberg, Tom, *Ruling Passions* (London: Jonathan Cape, 1977).

Drucker, Malka, *Frida Kahlo: Torment and Triumph* (New York: Bantam Books, 1991).

Evans, Richard, *The Third Reich at War, 1939–1945* (London: Allen Lane, 2008).

Ferguson, Niall, *The House of Rothschild: The World's Banker 1849–1999* (New York: Viking, 1999).

Fleming, Michael, *Auschwitz, The Allies and Censorship of the Holocaust* (Cambridge: Cambridge University Press, 2014).

Fondation Beyeler, *Pierre Bonnard*, edited by Ulf Küster (Riehen/Basel, 2012).

Freedman, Lawrence, *Strategy: A History* (New York: Oxford University Press, 2013).

Friedländer, Saul, *The Years of Extermination: Nazi Germany and the Jews, 1939–1945* (New York: HarperCollins, 2007).

Friedman, B.H., *Jackson Pollock: Energy Made Visible* (New York: Da Capo Press, 1964).

Friedrich, Jörg, *The Fire: The Bombing of Germany, 1940–1945*, trans. by Allison Brown (New York: Columbia University Press, 2006).

Fuechtner, Veronika, Douglas Haynes & Ryan M. Jones, *A Global History of Sexual Science 1880–1960* (Berkeley: University of California Press, 2018).

Gaglione, Anthony, *The United Nations under Trygve Lie, 1945–1953* (Lanham, MD: Scarecrow Press, 2001).

Galbraith, John Kenneth, *A Life in our Times* (Boston: Houghton Mifflin, 1981).

Gathorne-Hardy, Jonathan, *Sex, The Measure of All Things: A Life of Alfred Kinsey* (Bloomington: Indiana University Press, 2000).

Gilbert, James, *Men in the Middle: Searching for Masculinity in the 1950s* (Chicago: University of Chicago Press, 2005).

Gilbert, Martin, *Churchill: A Life* (New York: Henry Holt, 1992).

Gildea, Robert, *Fighters in the Shadows: A New History of the French Resistance* (Cambridge: Harvard University Press, 2015).

Gillin, Donald G., & Ramon H. Myers (eds), trans. by Dolores Zen, *Last Chance in Manchuria: The Diary of Chang Kia-Ngau* (Stanford, CA: Hoover Institution Press, 1989).

Glynn, Paul, *A Song for Nagasaki* (London: Fount Paperbacks, 1990).

Goossen, Rachel Waltner, *Women against the Good War: Conscientious Objection and Gender on the American Home Front, 1941–1947* (Chapel Hill: University of North Carolina Press, 1997).

Gordon-Reed, Annette, *Race on Trial* (New York: Oxford University Press, 2002).

Gourse, Leslie, *Sassy: The Life of Sarah Vaughan* (New York: Charles Scribner's Sons, 1993).

Guillain, Robert, *I Saw Tokyo Burning: An Eyewitness Narrative from Pearl Harbor to Hiroshima* (Garden City, New York: Doubleday, 1982).

Hachiya, Michihiko, *Hiroshima Diary*, ed. and trans. by Warner Wells (Chapel Hill: University of North Carolina Press, 1955).

Ham, Paul, *Hiroshima Nagasaki* (London: Doubleday, 2012).

Hamilton, Nigel, *JFK: Reckless Youth* (New York: Random House, 1992).

Hareven, Tamara K., *Eleanor Roosevelt: An American Conscience* (Chicago: Quadrangle Books, 1968).

Harrer, Heinrich, *Seven Years in Tibet* (New York: Putnam, 1996).

Hartman, J. Ted, *Tank Driver: With the Eleventh Armored from the Battle of the Bulge to VE Day* (Bloomington: Indiana University Press, 2003).

Harvey, Robert, *American Shogun: MacArthur, Hirohito, and the American Duel with Japan* (London: John Murray, 2006).

Hastings, Max, *Armageddon: The Battle for Germany, 1944–1945* (London: Macmillan, 2004).

Hauge, Jens Chr, *The Liberation of Norway* (Oslo: Gyldendal Norsk Forlag, 1995).

Hedges, Jill, *Evita* (London and New York: I.B. Tauris, 2017).

Herrera, Hayden, *Frida Kahlo: The Paintings* (New York: HarperCollins, 1991).

Hicks, George, *The Comfort Women: Japan's Brutal Regime of Enforced Prostitution in the Second World War* (New York: W.W. Norton, 1995).

Higonnet, Margaret (ed.), *Behind the Lines: Gender and the Two World Wars* (New Haven, CT: Yale University Press, 1987).

Ho Chi Minh, 'Declaration of Independence' in Gregory Allen Olson (ed.), *Landmark Speeches on the Vietnam War* (College Station: Texas A&M University Press, 2010).

Holloway, David, *Stalin and the Bomb* (New Haven, CT: Yale University Press, 1994).

Holman, Dennis, *Lady Louis: Life of the Countess Mountbatten of Burma* (London: Odhams Limited Press, 1952).

Hyman, Timothy, *Bonnard* (London: Thames & Hudson, 1998).

Ignatieff, Michael, *Isaiah Berlin: A Life* (New York: Metropolitan Books, 1998).

Isenberg, Noah, *We'll always have Casablanca: The Life, Legend, and Afterlife of Hollywood's Most Beloved Movie* (New York: W.W. Norton, 2017).

Jackson, Ashley, *Botswana, 1939–1945: An African Country at War* (Oxford: Clarendon Press, 1999).

Jaern, Albert, *And Then Came the Liberators*, trans. by Solveig Schavland (Madison, WI: Borderland Books, 2001).

Jayakar, Pupul, *Indira Gandhi: A Biography* (New Delhi, 1992).

Jones, James H., *Alfred C. Kinsey: A Public/Private Life* (New York: W.W. Norton, 1997).

Judt, Tony, *Postwar: A History of Europe Since 1945* (London: Penguin Press, 2005).

Kahlo, Frida, *The Diary of Frida Kahlo: An Intimate Self-Portrait* (New York: Harry N. Abrams, 1995).

Kennedy, Paul, *The Parliament of Man: The Past, Present, and Future of the United Nations* (New York: Random House, 2006).

Kennez, Peter, *Hungary from the Nazis to the Soviets: The Establishment of the Communist Regime in Hungary, 1944–1948* (New York: Cambridge University Press, 2006).

Klinger, William, & Denis Kuljiš, *Tito's Secret Empire: How the Maharaja of the Balkans Fooled the World* (Oxford: Oxford University Press, 2021).

Knappe, Siegfried, with Ted Brusaw, *Soldat: Reflections of a German Soldier, 1936–1949* (New York: Orion Books, 1992).

Kochendoerfer, Violet, *One Woman's World War II* (Lexington: University Press of Kentucky, 1994).

Krylova, Anna, *Soviet Women in Combat: A History of Violence on the Eastern Front* (New York: Cambridge University Press, 2010).

Kurosawa, Akira, *Something Like an Autobiography* (New York: Knopf, 1982)

LaFeber, Walter, *America, Russia and the Cold War, 1945–2002* (New York: McGraw-Hill, 2002).

Lanzona, Vina, *Amazons of the Huk Rebellion: Gender, Sex, and Revolution in the Philippines* (Madison: University of Wisconsin Press, 2009).

Lary, Diana, *The Chinese People at War: Human Suffering and Social Transformation, 1937–1945* (New York: Cambridge University Press, 2010).

Leckie, Robert, *Okinawa: The Last Battle of World War II* (New York: Viking Press, 1995).

Lefebvre, Michel, & Bernard Lebrun, *Robert Capa: The Paris Years 1933–1954* (New York: Harry N. Abrams, 2012).

Leymarie, Jean, *Picasso: The Artist of the Century* (New York: Viking Press, 1972).

Litoff, J.B., & D.C. Smith (eds), *Since You Went Away* (Oxford: Oxford University Press, 1991).

Loringhoven, Bernd Freytag von, *In the Bunker with Hitler: The Last Witness Speaks* (London: Weidenfeld & Nicolson, 2007).

Lottman, Herbert R., *The French Rothschilds: The Great Banking Dynasty Through Two Turbulent Centuries* (New York: Crown, 1995).

Lowrie, Donald A., *The Hunted Children* (New York: W.W. Norton, 1963).

Lusseyran, Jacques, *Et la lumière fut* (Chatou: Les Trois Arches, 1987).

Manchester, William, & Paul Reid, *The Last Lion* (Boston: Little, Brown and Company, 2012).

Mandela, Nelson, *Long Walk to Freedom* (Boston: Little, Brown and Company, 1994).

Marling, Karal Ann, & John Wetenhall, *Iwo Jima: Monuments, Memories, and the American Hero* (Cambridge, MA: Harvard University Press, 1991).

Marton, Kati, *Wallenberg* (New York: Random House, 1982).

Marx, Joseph L., *Seven Hours to Zero* (New York, Putnam, 1967).

Masson, Madeleine, *Edwina: The Biography of the Countess Mountbatten of Burma* (London: R. Hale, 1958).

Mayo, Jonathan, & Emma Craigie, *Hitler's Last Day Minute by Minute* (London: Octopus, 2016).

Meacham, Jon, *Franklin and Winston* (New York: Random House, 2003).

Melody, M.E., & Linda M. Peterson, *Teaching America About Sex: Marriage Guides and Sex Manuals from the Late Victorians to Dr. Ruth* (New York: New York University Press, 1999).

Meredith, Martin, *Nelson Mandela* (New York: Public Affairs, 2010).

Miller, Donald L., *Masters of the Air* (New York: Simon and Schuster, 2006).

Montefiore, Simon Sebag, *Stalin: The Court of the Red Tsar* (New York: Alfred A. Knopf, 2004).

Morgan, Janet, *Edwina Mountbatten: A Life of Her Own* (London: HarperCollins, 1991).

Myers, John Bernard, *Tracking the Marvelous: A Life in the New York Art Word* (New York: Random House, 1983).

Naifeh, Steven, & Gregory White Smith, *Jackson Pollock: An American Saga* (New York: C.N. Potter, 1989).

Neal, Steve, *Eleanor and Harry: The Correspondence of Eleanor Roosevelt and Harry S. Truman* (New York: Scribner, 2002).

Neave, Alex, *On Trial at Nuremberg* (Boston: Little, Brown and Company, 1978).

Niven, Bill (ed.), *Die Wilhelm Gustloff: Geschichte und Erinnerung eines Untergangs* (Halle: Mitteldeutscher Verlag, 2011).

Norman, Elizabeth M., *We Band of Angels: The Untold Story of American Nurses Trapped on Bataan by the Japanese* (New York: Random House, 1999).

O'Brien, Michael, *John F. Kennedy* (New York: Thomas Dunne Books, 2005).

Ohnuki-Tierney, Emiko, *Kamikaze Diaries: Reflections of Japanese Student Soldiers* (Chicago: University of Chicago Press, 2006).

Ortiz, Alicia Dujovne, & Shawn Fields, *Eva Perón* (New York: St. Martins Press, 1996).

Overy, Richard, *Goering* (London: Routledge & Kegan Paul, 1984).

Page, Suzanne (ed.), *Pierre Bonnard: The Work of Art* (Ghent: Ludion Press, 2006).

Page, Tim (ed.), *The Diaries of Dawn Powell, 1931–1965* (South Royalton, VT: Steerforth Press, 1998).

Perón, Eva, *My Mission in Life* (New York: Vantage Press, 1953).

Phibbs, Brendan, *The Other Side of Time: A Combat Surgeon in WWII* (Boston: Little, Brown, and Company, 1987).

Piccigallo, Philip, *The Japanese on Trial: Allied War Crimes Operations in the East (1945–1961)* (Austin: University of Texas Press, 1979).

Plokhy, S.M., *Yalta: The Price of Peace* (New York: Penguin Books, 2011).

Prince, Cathryn J., *Death in the Baltic: The World War II Sinking of the Wilhelm Gustloff* (New York: Palgrave Macmillan, 2013).

Rickman, Jon T., & Kim D. Todd, *Pioneer Programmer: Jean Jennings Bartik and the Computer that Changed the World* (Kirksville, MS: Truman State University Press, 2020).

Ridley, Jasper, *Tito* (London: Constable, 1994).

Roberts, Andrew, *Masters and Commanders: How Roosevelt, Churchill, Marshall and Allanbrooke Won the War in the West* (London: Allen Lane, 2008).

Roberts, Geoffrey, *Stalin's War: From World War to Cold War, 1939–1953* (New Haven, CT: Yale University Press, 2006).

Robien, Beata de, *La malédiction de Svetlana* (Paris: Albin Michel, 2016).

Rudel, Hans Ulrich, *Stuka Pilot* (New York: Bantam Books, 1979).

Saffle, Sue (ed.), *To the Bomb and Back: Finnish Children Tell their World War II Stories* (New York and Oxford: Berghahn Books, 2015).

Sands, Phillippe, *East West Street* (New York: Vintage, 2016).

Scammell, Michael, *Solzhenitsyn* (London: Paladin, 1986).

Schön, Heinz, *Die Gustloff Katastrophe: Bericht eines Überlebenden* (Stuttgart: Motorbuch Verlag, 2002).

Sebag Montefiore, Simon, *Stalin: The Court of the Red Tsar* (New York: Knopf, 2004).

Sellwood, Arthur V., *The Damned Don't Drown: The Sinking of the Wilhelm Gustloff* (Annapolis, MD: Naval Institute Press, 1996).

Serraller, F.C., & J. Semprun (eds), *Picasso: Tradition and Avant-Garde* , *Picasso: Tradition and Avant-Garde: 6 June–4 September 2006* (Exhibition catalogue, Madrid: Museo Nacional del Prado, 2006).

Shtemenko, S.M., *The Last Six Months: Russia's Final Battles with Hitler's Armies in World War II* (Garden City, NY: Doubleday, 1977).

Silverman, Jonathan, *For the World to See: The Life of Margaret Bourke-White* (New York: Viking, 1983).

Silverman, Kenneth, *Begin Again: A Biography of John Cage* (Evanston: Northwestern University Press, 2012).

Sinclair, Charlotte, *Vogue on Christian Dior* (New York: Abams Image, 2014).

Sisman, Adam, *An Honourable Englishman* (New York: Random House, 2010).

Sisulu, Walter & Albertina, *In Our Lifetime* (London: Abacus, 2003).

Sloan, Bill, *The Ultimate Battle: Okinawa 1945: The Last Epic Struggle of World War II* (New York: Simon & Schuster, 2008).

Soames, Mary (ed.), *Winston and Clementine: The Personal Letters of the Churchills* (New York: Doubleday, 1998).

Solzhenitsyn, Alexander, *The Gulag Archipelago*, Vol. I (London: Fantana/Collins, 1982).

Somerhausen, Anne, *Written in Darkness: A Belgian Woman's Record of the Occupation 1940–1945* (New York, 1946).

Speer, Albert, *Inside the Third Reich: Memoirs* (New York: MacMillan, 1970).

Stettinius, Edward, *Roosevelt and the Russians* (Garden City, NY: Doubleday, 1949).

Steve, Bruce M., & Michelle Palmer with Frank Present, *Witnesses to Nuremberg: An Oral History* (West Hartford, CT: Kumarian Press, 1998).

Sullivan, Rosemary, *The Extraordinary and Tumultuous Life of Stalin's Daughter* (New York: Harper, 2015).

Summers, Anthony, *Goddess: The Secret Lives of Marilyn Monroe* (New York: MacMillan, 1985).

Tanaka, Toshiyuki, *Hidden Horrors: Japanese War Crimes in World War II* (Boulder, CO: Westview, 1996).

Taylor, Julie M., *Eva Perón: The Myths of a Woman* (Chicago: University of Chicago Press, 1979).

Taylor, Telford, *The Anatomy of the Nuremberg Trials* (New York: Knopf, 1992).

Tibbets, Paul W., *The Tibbets Story* (New York: Stein and Day, 1978).

Totani, Yuma, *Justice in Asia and the Pacific Region, 1945–1952: Allied War Crimes Prosecutions* (Cambridge: Cambridge University Press, 2015).

Trial of the Major War Criminals before the International Military Tribunal, Washington DC, 14 November 1945–1 October 1946 (The Avalon Project: avalon.law.yale.edu/subject_menus/imt.asp).

Ulam, Adam, *Stalin: The Man and his Era* (New York: Viking Press, 1973).

Van der Rol, Ruud, & Rian Verhoeven, *Anne Frank: Beyond the Diary* (New York: Viking Press, 1993).

Van der Zee, Henri, *The Hunger Winter: Occupied Holland 1944–1945* (Lincoln: University of Nebraska Press, 1998).

Wallace, Chris, with Mitch Weiss, *Countdown 1945: The Extraordinary Story of the Atomic Bomb and the 116 Days that Changed the World* (New York: Avid Reader Press, 2020).

Walzer, Michael, *Just and Unjust Wars: A Moral Argument with Historical Illustrations* (New York: Basic Books, 2006).

Weinberg, Gerhard L., *Visions of Victory: The Hopes of Eight World War II Leaders* (New York: Cambridge University Press, 2005).

Weld, Jacqueline Bograd, *Peggy: The Wayward Guggenheim* (New York:

Dutton, 1986).

West, Richard, *Tito and the Rise and Fall of Yugoslavia* (London: Sinclair-Stevenson, 1994).

Wheelan, Joseph, *Bloody Okinawa: The Last Great Battle of World War II* (New York: Hachette Books, 2020).

Wiesen Cook, Blanche, *Eleanor Roosevelt: The War Years and after 1939–1962*, Vol. 3 (New York: Viking, 2016).

Wilcox, Claire, & Circe Henestrosa, *Frida Kahlo: Making Herself Up* (London: V&A Publishing, 2018).

Williams, Susan, *Spies in the Congo: America's Atomic Mission in World War II* (New York: Public Affairs, 2014).

Wilson, Elizabeth, *Rostropovich* (Chicago: Ivan R. Dee, 2008).

Woolner, David B., *The Last 100 Days* (New York: Basic Books, 2017).

Yad Vashem, Righteous Among the Nations (www.yadvashem.org/righteous/stories/wallenberg.html).

Yahara, Hiromichi, *The Battle for Okinawa* (New York: J. Wiley, 1995).

Young-Bruehl, Elisabeth, *Anna Freud* (New Haven, CT: Yale University Press, 2008).

Zaloga, Steven J., *Panther vs Sherman: Battle of the Bulge 1944* (Oxford: Osprey, 2008).

Zeiler, Thomas, W., & Daniel M. Dubois (eds), *A Companion to World War II* (Hoboken, NJ: Wiley-Blackwell, 2013).

Ziegler, Philip, *Mountbatten* (London: Collins, 1985).

Zolotow, Maurice, *Marilyn Monroe* (New York: Harper Perennial, 1990).

Acknowledgments

This book is the product of many minds and generous contributions. First, I extend my gratitude to the memoirists whose courageous testimonies continue to illuminate the past, offering both understanding and warning to future generations.

My research on 1945 would not have been possible without the support of the University of Washington Libraries – particularly the Suzzallo, Allen, and Art Libraries – as well as the photographic divisions of NARA (College Park, Maryland) and The Franklin D. Roosevelt Presidential Library (Hyde Park, New York). Laurie Austin at The Harry S. Truman Presidential Library (Independence, Missouri) played a crucial role in enhancing photographic quality and clarifying copyright issues. I am also grateful to the Australian War Memorial and The National Archives of Norway.

The intellectual generosity of scholars has been indispensable. Julian Graffy's insights into the Great Patriotic War and Communist culture, Alexis Klimoff's expertise on Solzhenitsyn and reflections on his own family's past, and Neil Carrick's knowledge of the intelligentsia – along with his early encouragement – have all shaped this work in profound ways.

Friends and colleagues provided invaluable feedback, refining and strengthening this book at every stage. I am deeply thankful to Dennis Carroll, Mark Watson, Andrew Connolly, Brian Walker, Garry Hamilton, Brian Alkire, Bill Neighbor, Robert Foxcurran, Francine Marx, Dexter Marx (no relation), David Weisberg, Quentin Van Doosselaere, Karla Rielau, and Bernard Wathelet.

I also would like to thank a group of friends in London for our thoughtful discussions over decades, and encouragements to persevere: Spyros Economides, Hugh C. Dyer, Fernando Guimaraes, Heinrich Senfft, and Tony Fenner-Leitao. Special thanks to Leon Mangasarian, whose meticulous proofreading brought clarity and precision to the manuscript. His generosity extended beyond the text itself: through him, I gained access to letters from his wife Tatjana's family archive, including a deeply moving 1 January 1945 letter from her grandfather, Graf Hohenthal-Püchau, mourning his son's death and foreseeing the loss of his estate. These connections across time and experience reaffirm the shared nature of history.

I have been exceptionally fortunate in my professional partnerships. My agent, Robert Dudley, has provided steadfast guidance, while Claire Hartley at The History Press brought remarkable creativity and efficiency to the publication process. I am also grateful to cover designer Katie Beard, layout designer Anita Pumfrey, copyeditor Sarah Wright, and proofreader Rebecca Newton, whose expertise transformed the manuscript into its final form.

Finally, my deepest thanks go to my family. My wife, Nancy, whose love and empathy have sustained me throughout, and our daughters, Adele and Leah: may you always recognize the interwoven nature of our lives and cherish peace as the highest good.